50p

REVOLT FROM T

37

REVOLT
FROM THE CENTER

Niels I. Meyer, K. Helveg Petersen and
Villy Sørensen

Translated by Christine Hauch

MARION BOYARS
LONDON · BOSTON

Published in Great Britain and the United States in 1981
by Marion Boyars Publishers Ltd.
18 Brewer Street London W1R 4AS
and Marion Boyars Publishers Inc.
99 Main Street, Salem, New Hampshire 03079

First published in Denmark in 1978
by Gyldendalske Boghandel, Nordisk Forlag A.S., Copenhagen
as *Oprør fra midten*

© Gyldendalske Boghandel, Nordisk Forlag A.S., Copenhagen 1978
© This translation Marion Boyars Publishers Ltd. 1981

Australian and New Zealand distribution by Thomas C. Lothian
4-12 Tattersalls Lane, Melbourne, Victoria 3000

British Library Cataloguing in Publication Data

Meyer, Neils I.
    Revolt from the center. – (Open forum).
    1. Civilization , Occidental
    2. Civilization, Modern – 1950-
    I. Title   II. Petersen, K. Helveg
    III. Sorenson, Villy   IV. Series
    909'098120828   CB245   79-56838

ISBN cloth 0-7145-2701-7
ISBN paper 0-7145-2702-5
Library of Congress Catalog Card Number 79-56838

ALL RIGHTS RESERVED
Any paperback edition of this book whether published simultaneously with, or subsequent to, the cased edition is sold subject to the condition that it shall not, by way of trade, be lent, resold, hired out, or otherwise disposed of, without the publisher's consent, in any form of binding or cover other, than that in which it was published.

No part of this publication may be reproduced, stored in a retrieval system, or transmitted, in any form or by any means, electronic, mechanical, photocopying, recording or otherwise, except brief extracts for the purposes of review, without the prior written permission of the publisher.

Set in VIP Palatino by John Smith, London
Printed and bound in Great Britain by
Redwood Burn Limited
Trowbridge & Esher

CONTENTS

PREFACE TO THE ENGLISH EDITION

Revolt from the Center was first published in Denmark in February 1978 and gave rise to a heated and lasting political debate in the Danish mass media. The reactions illustrated the acute interest for an alternative to the traditional Western type of industrial society.

In some parts of the book Denmark has been used as a concrete example for discussion and analysis. This does not prevent the conclusions we reach from being equally valid in a wider context since the social structure of Denmark is very much akin to that of the other Western industrial nations. It is worth pointing out, however, that since 1973 there have been around ten political parties represented in the Danish parliament and this has made the very business of problem-solving problematical. There was a renaissance of Marxism after the youth movement of 1968, and in 1973 Mogens Glistrup led a right-wing rebellion against the burden of taxation and state bureaucracy. Between the opposing wings of rebellion the centre parties – which in Denmark include the ruling social democratic party – were forced into a defensive position from which it was impossible to conduct a policy that would effectively overcome the crises of the 1970s.

But the book is not intended merely to be an appeal to the democratic centre parties; it is also, and more particularly, a challenge to the great democratic majority which does not support, indeed recoils from, the extreme solutions proposed by the left- and right-wing parties. The problems affecting Europe cannot be solved by traditional means: when considering future development we must look not only for new paths but also for a new goal. The old political ideologies liberalism and marxism which arose in the 18th and 19th centuries respectively are inadequate in the late 20th century. They share a common faith in

7

development, a belief that economic growth is a prerequisite of democratic evolution. The recognition that there are limits to growth has reinforced the need for an up-to-date ideology. The recognition that economic growth in the wealthy countries has done nothing to reduce the gap between rich and poor nations but has rather increased it, suggests an ideology that is not primarily rooted in economic interests. The new ideology must be rooted in those human needs which it is hard to fulfil in modern industrial society.

All these common problems are, of course, common to large and small nations alike. And all nations share a preoccupation with their own difficulties which leaves them no time to devote to the wider perspectives. In this respect Denmark is no less guilty than any other country, and the fact that it is small is no excuse. Smaller nations may be more dependent on larger nations but their opportunities for change are better than those of the bigger countries. Denmark has just over 5 million inhabitants – half the population of New York. If it is not possible to create conditions there in which the citizens can feel *at ease* and for which they assume joint responsibility, then it is not possible to do so anywhere. The ideas concerning decentralization, participation and protection of the environment which are common to many of the new movements of the 1970s cannot be put into practice by directives from above: protest against the large units must proceed from the smaller – on an international level the small nations share common interests in relation to the superpowers.

Revolt from the Center is an attempt to establish and to justify a new goal for social development. We should stress that the future society outlined in Chapter IV is not intended to be either a prediction of the future – which will doubtless turn out quite differently – or a definitive ideal: it is an attempt to show how the kind of society heralded by many new movements in Denmark and elsewhere might look. We do not regard it as a shortcoming that many of the points made in this book have also been covered in other works – what may be new here is in the main the attempt to describe a consistent and integrated solution.

One of the chief barriers to the development of a humane sustainable society is the increasing dependence of politicians on experts who are generally interested in progress being concentrated in their own areas of specialization. It was in order to counteract this tendency, among other reasons, that the three of us, a physicist, a politician and a philosopher combined to write this book.

Niels I. Meyer
K. Helveg Petersen
Villy Sørensen

FOREWORD TO THE DANISH EDITION

A foreword often acts as a concealed excuse. Concealment is not necessary, excuses do no harm. Our excuse for taking three of us to write this book is that none of us could have written it alone. Our excuse for writing what many other people have written as well is that, as far as we know, there is no work which combines a critical analysis of modern – and in particular Danish – industrial society with a political programme based on a detailed (and not just an implied or inferred) perception of human beings. Apart from the fact that some of the ideas in this book may possibly be our own, what is new – and ambitious – about it is the combination.

We have a notion of how society should be arranged so as to give people the best fulfilment. We also have some notions of how such a society could be realized, though we do not deceive ourselves, or anyone else, that it will be easy. We have considered it useful to sketch a future society that is not *too* utopian to be realizable. Our future society is influenced to a great extent by our present one and, if nothing else, it is at least well-suited to show up the shady side of present society more clearly – or rather more darkly.

One more apology is necessary. This is directed to all those splendid people – politicians, civil servants, experts and organization men – who are putting enormous, sometimes inhuman, efforts into making an antiquated politico-economic system work. Our pet hypothesis is that the faults lie not in people but elsewhere. We are aware of the dangers allied to over-destructive criticism of existing society, the kind of criticism which spares nothing, not even what deserves to endure. But we are also aware of the danger of defending everything that exists because

11

some of it deserves to endure – and of leaving more radical criticism to those who will preserve nothing.

One of us has associations with a political party. We should perhaps point out, therefore, that we do not use the word 'radical' in a party political sense and that the views and suggestions in this book are not a party political programme – although we naturally have nothing against the political parties taking it up if only to criticize. We would rather be criticized for opinions we hold than for those we do not hold.

Niels I. Meyer
K. Helveg Petersen
Villy Sørensen

CHAPTER ONE

THE BACKGROUND

BOOM OR BANKRUPTCY?

In the post-war period Western industrial societies have achieved a prosperity unprecedented in history. This increased affluence in the last thirty years has not led to greater social and spiritual harmony but to greater discord. We have reached a point at which our boom society is beginning to look very much like a bankrupt society. Many industrial nations have built up debts which limit their political freedom of action. The unemployment problem which economic and political experts thought they had wiped out only a few years ago is now regarded as insoluble. The inability of governments and parliaments to solve these problems has undermined confidence in the effectiveness of the democratic parliamentary system itself.

A surprisingly short time ago it was common enough to hear the phrase 'we've never had it so good'; and then, in the 'swinging sixties' it was still possible to feel that good times could be even better. But the higher the standard of living, the more difficult it becomes to achieve any noticeable progress. The satisfaction of basic needs brings basic satisfaction. The acquisition of things that are not needed is less gratifying and so demands for them increase. We have fallen into the habit of regarding continuous economic growth as a law of nature, and of seeing continuous material improvement as a basic human right. This is why the recession of recent years has increased the general sense of frustration.

We are not saying that dissatisfaction itself is the major problem in an industrial society but rather the abuses on which discontent is based. A distinctive feature of the material progress

13

of the last decades has been that things become obsolete long before they are worn out. Economic expansion is powered by the superpowers and the multinationals as they race to be first to exploit new avenues of technology. The crucial question asked about such innovations is not how they will profit mankind but what profit can be made from them; and this applies equally to armaments, technical products and everyday consumer goods. If the consumer is to continue wanting new products he must continue to feel dissatisfied with the old. It is therefore no mere coincidence that increasing prosperity is accompanied by increasing dissatisfaction. Dissatisfaction with what is currently available is both a product and a pre-condition of continuous growth in production.

Even a few years ago there was still a general assumption that we could produce our way out of inequality and poverty, and it is still generally assumed that growth in production and consumption is the only way out of unemployment. Increased prosperity in the wealthy countries, however, has brought no corresponding benefits to the poor. Indeed, the processes of under-development and over-development are one and the same. Up until now we have looked upon the natural world as raw material for human enterprise rather than as the foundation of our existence, and we have treated it accordingly. But the evidence that we are in danger of destroying the natural world and creating imminent shortages of essential resources has made it obvious that the uncontrolled growth of production and consumption creates greater problems of scarcity than any it solves.

While we may recognize the limits to growth, there are no signs that this recognition can be translated into effective political action, although we know that time is short. On the contrary, the aggravated conflicts in society brought about by economic recession suggest that we must have economic growth for parliamentary democracy to work. Economic crises lead to political crises and it becomes questionable whether in such crises effective government can actually be combined with democracy.

FATAL CONTRADICTIONS

It is easy enough to see the necessity for radical change on both national and international levels; it is more difficult to see the possibility of such change occurring. The atmosphere of conflict which pervades the international situation emerges as a string of fatal contradictions:

1. Economic growth leads to shortage problems.
2. Development has resulted both in greater discrepancies and in greater interdependence between nations.
3. The major problems can only be solved on an international level; there are no effective international institutions; national governments can only try to keep pace with development.
4. Measures for peaceful change must come from the wealthy 25% of the world's population which consumes 75% of its resources. But the rich nations are most interested in maintaining international class divisions.
5. Growing hardship in the developing countries and the demands of industrialized countries for raw materials are increasing the danger of conflict. World expenditure on armaments is fifteen times as high as the entire amount given in aid to developing nations, while military expenditure accounts for a rising proportion of the national product in these countries.
6. The further off any impending disaster appears the weaker the incentive to avert it; the closer the disaster the weaker the chance of averting it.
7. The more urgent the problems are the more dictatorial any counter-measures become. The only defence against dictatorial 'solutions' is effective democracy; the more critical the situation the less effective the democracy.
8. Awareness of problems does not automatically lead to action. We prefer to remain in ignorance of problems we can do little about; no one likes waking up to a bad dream.

BELIEF IN DEVELOPMENT
AND CRISIS OF CONFIDENCE

At one time people were prepared to believe in something they did not know for a fact. Nowadays it appears that we are not prepared to believe in what we know all too well. We may be fully aware that development can lead to shortage but we cannot really believe it.

Belief is confidence in the ruling powers; a harmonious social order is generally anchored in belief of this kind. The Christian

15

Church, particularly in Roman Catholic countries, has often joined forces with the state in maintaining law and order in society; but the belief that social order was rooted in a divine world order has long since been undermined by scientific, technical and economic development, and has now been superseded by belief in that development itself. Although it has assumed various guises, this belief in economic development has been the dominant faith in Europe and North America since the industrial revolution. It reached a peak in the wave of affluence following the war and has been badly shaken during the economic and ecological crises of recent years.

A crisis of confidence sets in with the first glimmerings of awareness that there is no superior reasoning power behind development but only human reason or lack of it. The political leaders who have attracted the most fervent following have been those who were regarded as the instruments of providence or history and therefore to a larger extent infallible. The greatest scepticism is reserved for the elected leaders whom it is much harder to credit with some superior wisdom. And it appears that people today do still need to believe in some wisdom superior to their own; a primitive outlook perhaps but rational enough considering how little wisdom people manifest themselves. Political leaders are quite likely to be held responsible for the general drift of events, but even so they are not credited with any real authority over things. Power is broken down into a number of impersonal, unseen powers. The faith in experts is much greater (they at least know things which are usually well beyond our comprehension); but there is also a stronger tendency to challenge their infallibility.

REVOLT FROM THE LEFT AND THE RIGHT – AND FROM THE CENTER

In 1964 Herbert Marcuse wrote a celebrated book about the one-dimensional man who cannot see any alternative to existing society. If development itself is a matter of belief there is no reason to reverse it. To find dissenting views we must look to those who are not established members of society, and in particular to the young whose opportunities to influence the course of modern society are delayed for increasing lengths of time as their period of education is prolonged. In this sense Marcuse foreshadowed the youth movement that broke out in rebellion a few years later.

Many of the young people who were being raised to take over the future reacted against that future. They could not know from personal experience that the times had improved and were getting still better. On the contrary, they had been educated to expect more of modern society. And they were the first to rebel against that belief in Development which Development itself was calling into question.

Material advances have not ironed out the differences between rich and poor on either the national or the international level. Theoretically political development has given everyone a share in government, but in reality it has made the authorities even more distant. Social advances have given individuals greater security but have also torn them away from the fellowship of smaller communities. When viewed in terms of the arms race, environmental pollution and ruthless exploitation of natural resources, scientific and technical advances have created greater problems than those they have solved. The welfare state can boast of a growing number of psychological ailments apparently caused by the pattern of society itself.

Behind the youth movement lay an international setting of concern in the Western world about the Vietnam war. Until that point the Western world had generally been known as the free world, but it is now more widely and more accurately called the capitalist world. Against this background, then, the youth movement implied a considerable Marxist renaissance and contributed powerfully to a polarization in society very much in keeping with the Marxist doctrine of class struggle.

Since then much criticism of the state has come from liberals protesting against the rising burden of taxation and the spread of bureaucracy and state-ownership. An avowedly socialist economist, Jørgen S. Dich, asserted in his book *The Ruling Class (Den herskende klasse)* that the social progress reflected in a growing public sector had reached a point at which the benefits did not measure up to the investment and where further growth in welfare, health and education services would be of less advantage to society than to the state, i.e. public sector employees. Although Dich's analyses have been criticized by several state-

17

employed economists, they do correspond to the widespread feeling of 'not getting one's money's worth' and to the equally common experience that public offices are not primarily a means of serving the citizens but of keeping them in order; a self-aggrandizing system of administration.

What is valid on an international level is also valid on a national level. The greater the problems of the community, the greater intolerance grows. Right-wingers talk of a left-wing bias in society; left-wingers of a right-wing bias; and although both sides tend to exaggerate the achievements of the other, extreme attitudes have been far more vigorously championed both inside and outside parliament in recent years. The extremist movements also have their patented solutions to the problems of society. One side says that the bureaucratic state must be dismantled and the public sector reduced. The other side demands nationalization of the means of production. The polls still indicate that the majority of people are unquestionably alarmed by these views. The fear of any radical solution whether left- or right-wing which might threaten our well-earned social benefits and bourgeois democracy remains an obstacle to social innovation. The old established parties are leaning inwards towards the center. And this means that the center is becoming a place where the opposing forces neutralize each other and stick to the time-honoured solutions instead of using it as a starting point for real innovation. Between the radical revolutionary movements the center parties are bogged down in a defence of what exists even though it cannot exist and be defended without change. What is needed, therefore, is a third revolt, from the center, a departure from rigid postures.

There should be no doubt that compromise and concession are crucial to democracy, but the compromise must be comprehensive enough to accommodate radical attitudes. A revolt from the center must strike both at forms of production governed by profit and at bureaucratic forms of government since both are incompatible with democracy.

ECONOMIC IDEOLOGIES

Naturally there are opposing economic interests underlying the polarization in society. But economic interests are generally justified with reference to society (e.g. what is good for the big companies is good for society) and justifications of this kind are very much like ideologies.

The two dominant political ideologies from which the right- and left-wing respectively take their bearings are essentially theories of economic development: liberalism was first presented in the 18th century as an argument for freedom of trade, marxism in the 19th century as a theory about the development and inevitable breakdown of capitalism. Both theories assume that human behaviour is economically motivated, that human thought is determined by economic interests (at least until the breakdown of the capitalist system). Despite the fact that the ideologies are economically motivated, ideology may still exert more control over people's thoughts and behaviour than their own real interests: ideological dogma can block our perception of reality.

Both liberalism and marxism are founded on scientific economic theories (inasmuch as economic theories can be scientific), but as ideologies they are still differing expressions of the belief in development, of confidence in those forces which govern development. This belief is clearly expressed in the creed of a free market economy steered by an 'invisible hand' which is described by Adam Smith, the father of liberalism. It is also expressed in the doctrines of Marx and marxism concerning the development of productive forces to a point at which they *demand* socialization of the means of production and in the stress they lay on the 'civilizing' role of capitalism. For dogmatic liberalism, as for dogmatic marxist-leninism, continuous growth is a precondition of the development of democracy and socialism respectively. 'Any rejection of the so-called " consumer society" which moves . . . to attack the historical extension of needs and consumption in general . . . turns back the clock from scientific to utopian socialism and from historical materialism to idealism' (Mandel, *Late Capitalism*). If there are limits to growth, there are also limits to the validity of growth ideologies in a situation radically divorced from the circumstances in which they first arose.

CRITIQUE OF LIBERALISM

Liberalism was originally a bourgeois-democratic countermovement to the privileges of rank and to trade restrictions.

From their beginning, the democratic ideas formulated in the declarations of human rights in the late 18th century were an expression both of economic interests (i.e. the right of every citizen to freely compete on an equal footing) and of a demand for justice (i.e. people's position in society must depend not on birth and inheritance but on their own efforts). There is thus a historical connection between economic liberalism and political democracy, though not a logical or necessary one. It is still generally assumed nevertheless, that democratic freedom implies economic freedom and that the right to private ownership of the means of production is an essential democratic right.

Old liberal dogma tells us that the welfare of every person is best served by every person working in his or her own best interests and that freedom of competition and freedom of consumer choice (the market mechanism) ensure maximum efficiency in production. Obviously this can only be true if every person *is* working in his or her own interest rather than selling his labour to others and if those who are freely competing on the market are near enough equally large and strong. Freedom of competition in itself leads to economic inequality and in practice economic freedom remains the right of the stronger to expand at the expense of the weaker. Economic freedom is by no means a foundation for political democracy, but on the contrary an obstacle to it. The vital question affecting mankind as a whole, namely how our limited resources should be used, is decided in the main by a number of independent and anonymous private authorities who are not required to consider the social consequences of their decisions to any great extent. Society is left to answer for the consequences without being able to make its own choices. Production for profit, which might have served a purpose during the critical phase of industrialism, is socially irresponsible in a situation where the forces of production and destruction are more highly advanced and more closely interconnected. The question of social control of production is therefore urgent, especially as increased competition between the big companies for smaller profits is making them more and more dependent on the state. Should the democratic states be serving the companies, or should the companies be serving the democratic state? The answer is self-evident. There are still powerful interests backing the liberalist belief that democratic freedom is

20

dependent on freedom of competition, but they are not the interests of the great majority. Nevertheless the great majority of
private individuals identify more closely with private than with
public enterprise. Marxists may regard the state as the extended
arm of capital, but for most people it is more like an obstacle to
private enterprise. Most people are actually snared in the prejudices of liberalist ideology.

IDEOLOGICAL CRAMP

Because political freedom is severely restricted in so-called
socialist countries, it seems quite natural still to regard economic
freedom as closely connected to democratic freedom. Nationalization of the means of production has not led to management by
society but to control by the state. The totalitarian nature of
avowedly socialist states leads us to view the existing democracies as the only alternative to socialism, whether realized or
not. Socialism is associated with dictatorship, democracy with
liberalism or capitalism.

During the cold war this opposition of ideas became frozen
solid and prevented the development of a democratic socialism in
either East or West. The thaw which took place in the 1960s coincided with a wave of affluence; and this wave not only washed
away the more ideological questions (and with them the long
term problems lurking in the background) but also strengthened
the unequivocal belief in development common to liberalism and
marxism alike. The crises of recent years have again increased
the need for an improvement in democracy, but they have also
breathed new life into the outdated ideological confrontations.
The fact that the economic freedom of bourgeois society is so
obviously close to the law of the jungle leads marxist-leninists
to express contempt for all 'bourgeois' freedoms and even
for 'bourgeois' democracy; and this contempt leads the more
bourgeois in their turn to defend the whole of their existing social
system as democratic. For marxist-leninism, social democracy is
the 'democracy . . . that is led by party and state' (*The Basis of
Marxism-Leninism*). Thus marxist-leninist theory (and practice) is
just as great an obstacle to socialist democracy as a liberalist,
capitalist economy.

CRITIQUE OF MARXISM-LENINISM

The basic writings of marxism-leninism do not deal with socialism or communism but with capitalism and its inevitable collapse. According to Karl Marx the capitalist system will break
down when it has fulfilled its civilizing mission and no longer
serves its purpose, i.e. no longer permits the means of production to be used effectively. 'Centralization of the means of production and socialization reach a point where they become
incompatible with their capitalist integument. This integument is
burst asunder'. Hotter competition between fewer and larger
enterprises leads to an international class conflict between the
few who have and the many have-nots. The overwhelming
majority of people will then revolt, take over the means of production and bring them under social control. Nationalization
of the means of production is realized as dictatorship of the
proletariat; it is, however, only the first phase in the transition to
a communist society in which each person produces according to
ability and is rewarded according to need, and in which the free
development of the individual is a precondition for the free
development of all.

Apart from these propositions, there is little in the writings of
Marx and Engels about the communist society. It is taken for
granted that people will come into their rightful inheritance when
they are free of economic exploitation, but human rights and
needs have never formed a central part of marxist-leninist ideology or politics. Nowhere has the so-called dictatorship of the
proletariat, which is actually the dictatorship of the party or the
party leaders, actually dissolved into democracy. The attempt to
achieve this in Czechoslovakia was crushed by force. There are
many explanations and excuses for this. Of these the most crucial
point is that transition to socialization of the means of production
has not gone according to theory; it has not occurred in the in-
dustrially, economically *and* democratically developed countries
but in the less developed countries where the transition is bound
to be harder just because they are less developed.

Obviously the fact that the capitalist system has not yet col-
lapsed in the West is no guarantee that it will not collapse in the
future. It is still true that the system is accompanied by a regular

series of recessionary crises; it is also true that the system is not serving its purpose. It has been impossible to find solutions to problems of unemployment and management of resources, not to mention inequality, within the framework of the capitalist system.

Neither the theory nor the practice of marxism-leninism, however, has much to teach us about the transition to a politico-economic system that combines economic control with political democracy. It is hard to find any basis for a 'classic' revolution in a modern world where:

1. There is no one global socialist movement but two rival communist superpowers and several rival parties representing different brands of socialism.
2. The clash that exists is not the predicted revolutionary conflict between the capitalist minority and the proletariat majority either internationally or within the capitalist countries, but on the contrary a conflict between rich and poor nations.
3. The development of the means of production and destruction makes any violent transition to a peaceful world highly unlikely. If the situation becomes desperate enough to spark off a revolution there is very little hope of finding a way back to democracy.

It is indignation about injustice in connection with material need that powers the work of the revolutionary. In the rich countries there is no such 'revolutionary situation'. The free-for-all struggle which liberalism saw as a means of economic progress for all has not been superseded by the class struggle between the haves and the have-nots which marxism sees as a means of transition to the classless society. On the contrary, the liberal's free-for-all has become a general struggle between economic pressure groups and a general hostility between different sections and professions in society, between public and private sector employees, educationalists, academics and even politicians. In much of the Western world *consciousness* of one's own democratic rights is more fully developed than democracy. It seems unfair that some should earn more than others; demands for higher wages are based more on notions of self-respect than on real hardship. We are therefore doing very little to relieve hardship in the world at large. And the marxist view, that the internal conflicts which limit our freedom of action internationally are actually contributing to the international class struggle is surely a delusion.

REVISIONISM

It is possible to find marxist economic analyses of the 'internal contradictions of capitalism' very much to the point without accepting the whole of marxist-leninist ideology. Marxist-leninists, however, consider it 'revisionism' to deviate from the authorized doctrine and regard revisionism as a dangerous aberration. In any case they believe marxist theory to be so dynamic that no predictions of how people will behave in the communist society are possible, though the development of capitalism has been predicted once and for all and must follow its preordained path.

The word 'revisionism' is applied in particular to social-democratic reformist politics which can, in fact, take some of the credit for the material progress which has prevented the impoverishment of the working class. An example of social-democratic compromise between liberal and socialist economics is the 'state interventionism' advocated by the English economist J. M. Keynes during the 1930s' crisis. As he saw it, full employment could be restored by increasing production and consumption with the help of public investment. The public sector has not grown as a parasite on the production sector but rather acted as an auxiliary engine which boosts the economy by taking over those tasks which private enterprise finds non-profitable but which are nevertheless necessary for the profit of the private sector. The mixed economy which created the welfare state has to a certain extent upheld the system: social-democratic politicians are generally accused of being the tools of capitalism and so on. It is true that social-democratic governments have laid greater stress on preserving democracy than on paving the way for socialism. Not without reason: democracy is easier to subvert than the capitalist system, and experience makes them wary.

If the social democrats have not stuck to dialectical materialism, however, they have at least stuck to materialism. Ever-increasing growth has been both the goal and the pre-requisite of social-democratic reformist politics. The re-orientation towards a different set of values, which society can afford to make when the

level of affluence is high – and which it cannot afford not to make
– may also lead the social-democratic parties to revise their own
policies.

THE NEED FOR DEMOCRATIC IDEOLOGY

It is not only the economically motivated ideologies and their
anti-communist and anti-liberalist ideas respectively that stand
in the way of social liberalism or liberal socialism. But the persuasive power exercised by these ideologies and the absence of
an up-to-date democratic ideology both contribute to the lack of
any democratic vigour.

Economic problems are only one aspect of the general social
crisis. There is another aspect which politicians tend to disregard
despite clear evidence of its existence in such instances as the
welfare state's vast consumption of tranquilizers, stimulants and
analgesics. This is the psychological crisis; the feeling of confusion and meaninglessness and, for that matter, the over-
consumption which is an obvious substitute for the satisfaction
of real needs. A democratic ideology must seek its point of
departure in the needs of the people and not, as marxism-
leninism does, regard these needs as a consequence of social and
economic development (the implication being that people can
and must be made to conform to the needs of the state).

One facet of this psychological need is the desire for meaning,
for belief, which has been satisfied by religions and political
ideologies. Belief is a confidence in the forces behind development, a consciousness of collaborating in something that is working for you. Is it possible, in circumstances where we know that
development can lead to disaster, to believe in something other
than the ruling experts? Something other than the 'strong man'
who emerges to take command at some specific point and is then
deemed to be in possession of or in accord with higher powers? Is
it possible, simply, to believe in people or in democracy?

A more reasonable question might be: is it possible to believe in
a social order and a world order that is not in harmony with
nature and in which the natural needs of people are not fulfilled?
We know that the continued exploitation of nature is undermin-
ing our existence and that the continued oppression of people
makes that existence meaningless. If we want to believe in some

kind of future, we must believe in the possibility of a society which is in balance with its natural environment and in which the human being is not a passive object of external decisions and influences but an active, independent person whose freedom to develop is a precondition for the free development of everybody. It is not necessary to believe in the possibility of such a society, a humane, ecologically sustainable society, ever being created, in order to see that it is right to work towards it.

In the Western world, with our over-consumption, our sectionalism and our lack of either domestic or more universal solidarity, we are working away in the opposite direction. It is disgraceful that rich societies are unable to solve their own economic problems and are actually sponging off the poor nations. We may be able to excuse our inability to solve world problems; there is no excuse for our failure to solve national problems. Just as people are not solely products of society, so is the nation more than the social system. The fight against international capitalism will not be won by weakening the economy of the country – and making it more dependent on international capital. A conscious effort to solve our own problems and to achieve freedom of action at home and abroad is the only means of escape from the psychological poverty affecting society.

We have seen that international problems cannot be solved by some central authority from above, that real international collaboration must start in the individual nations, and despite, or rather because of, their comparative political weakness the small nations are less immovable and less encumbered than the big powers. If a small nation with a homogeneous population cannot govern itself, there is very little hope of an entire world of autonomous societies working together. The task of solving large, common problems unites – small problems divide both society and people.

The fact that the common problems are global in nature does not make it provincial on our part to start by tackling the 'luxury problems' of the Western world or even of our own nation – where those problems are not too great to be solved. In the present situation it is possible to see not only the symptoms of breakdown but also the signs of a breakaway. We shall attempt to contribute to a breakaway, to a revolt from the center by:

1. Showing that the solution to present problems demands a break with prevailing development trends (Chapter II).
2. Deriving a social and political goal from people's natural needs (Chapter III).
3. Sketching the broad outlines of a society in which these needs are recognized (Chapter IV).
4. Indicating possible routes towards this goal (Chapter V).

CHAPTER TWO

THE ARGUMENT FOR CHANGE

THERE IS A LIMIT

What is new about our present predicament is the recognition that our common reserves of vital resources are threatened with exhaustion. The only solution to this problem is the establishment of a society, or a world society, in balance with its natural environment. Expert opinion is unanimous that any form of growth dependent on ever-increasing consumption of energy and raw materials and on progressive pollution of the physical environment cannot continue. Heated discussions are being held on these subjects anyway, but on closer inspection we can see that the real point at issue is how much time we have left in which to change course. Characteristically, it is usually the economists who are most optimistic on our behalf. Many of them are still bogged down in the liberalist belief that things will sort themselves out: if there is a shortage of anything either some substitute will be found or the price will rise so that consumption is reduced. When it comes to vital raw materials, however, it is no solution to raise prices progressively as stocks are exhausted until the cost is prohibitive. To do them justice, even some of the deeply entrenched liberalist economists recognize that the market and price mechanism is not a suitable means of controlling the long-term exploitation of resources.

Using the term in a wider than purely religious sense, there must be a conversion from prevailing attitudes before there can be any change in policy. We must recognize that the fundamental values in life are not man-made but inherent in nature. We are still influenced by the liberalistic dogma that human labour is the source of all value while nature is merely the raw material for human enterprise. We are still influenced by the belief that there is an 'invisible' hand steering economic development, that it is a 'natural' process. In fact the opposite is true. Economic development has been accompanied by an artificial encroachment on nature; and it would be more accurate to speak of an 'invisible hand' governing the natural ecological system, though not so invisible that it cannot hit hard when certain bounds are transgressed.

The most fundamental of these bounds relates to climate. A rise of even a few degrees in the mean temperature of the earth's surface can result in incalculable consequences. We already know that all forms of energy consumption result in a heating of the atmosphere and that the burning of fossil fuels (i.e. oil, coal and natural gas) creates vast quantities of carbon dioxide which may prevent heat loss from the earth and lead to the so-called greenhouse effect. What we do not know is at what point these effects will become noticeable; physical interaction in the balanced atmospheric system is so complicated that it is impossible to construct a theoretical model capable of accurately predicting the sensitivity to further influence. If we just 'carry on regardless' as the saying goes, on the basis that our knowledge is incomplete, we will not discover how great a margin is needed until it is too late. Even in specific areas where we do know enough, that knowledge is insufficient to lead to action. We know that the ozone layer which absorbs some of the ultra-violet radiation from the sun is broken down by various substances, including those used in spray cans. Even a minor increase in ultra-violet radiation results in a heightened incidence of skin cancer; a more drastic increase might threaten plant and animal life and cause climatic changes. Nevertheless, it has not yet been possible to bring in a universal ban on the use of this substance in spray cans. The drama of mankind, doom-laden tragedy as it sometimes appears, is not without its farcical moments.

During normal operation, nuclear energy pollutes the atmosphere less than fossil fuels, but the radio-active waste and security problems it produces have immeasurable social consequences which it is inexcusable and irresponsible to hand on to posterity. A society, whether national or international, that is in balance with nature, must rely on sources of energy that are renewable and not limited in stock. As might be expected,

29

however, exploration of the applications of solar energy has been neglected to the advantage of nuclear energy development.

MORE PEOPLE – MORE POVERTY

One of the crucial barriers to any curb on world economic growth is a rapid rise in population numbers which makes it necessary to provide more and more things for more and more people. In this respect, however, the situation in rich countries is totally different from that in the poor. In Great Britain, East and West Germany population levels are falling. In Denmark the amount by which the birth rate exceeds the death rate is growing smaller; if present trends continue there will be fewer people in Denmark by the turn of the century, and by the end of the next century the population will be halved.

As far as the traditional philosophy of growth is concerned, this drop in population is a disaster since society will stagnate. What this trend clearly suggests, however, is that the wealthy countries must lead the way in creating an ecologically sustainable society: affluence is the best weapon against population growth. In several wealthy nations population growth has already had an adverse effect on the quality of life. Norwegians and Swedes may describe the sense of claustrophobia brought about by living in Holland; they yearn for a natural environment in which it is possible to move about freely away from surrounding people and cars. But millions of children are going to grow up in cities without ever experiencing the world of unspoilt nature where they can drink safely from lakes and streams – and they will be barely aware of what they are missing.

With their present rate of population growth the poor nations have no chance of achieving affluence. Even in those cases where effective population policies could be successfully imposed now, it would take several generations to halt growth. The reason for this, paradoxically, is that the average age in poor countries is low, and where children now form almost half the population in a couple of decades there will be more adults to bring yet more children into the world. At the same time it is the low life expectancy resulting from famine and disease which, for the moment at any rate, forms the most effective curb on population growth. Colombia, for example, which is not one of the poorest countries, has a population of 24 million (double the 1955 figure) and an infant mortality rate of roughly 90,000 a year. In the light of such statistics it may appear cynical to discuss the necessity of world-wide limitation on material growth; but it is also cynical to use suffering in the developing countries as an argument for continued economic growth in the wealthy ones. If a world society in ecological balance is to be realized, it must also be a society of world-wide equality, and this demands fundamental changes particularly in the political aims and structures of the wealthy nations. There is no reason why developing countries should show consideration for the whole world when the industrialized countries do not; there is, however, every reason to fear that if present development continues the desperate conditions in many developing countries will produce ruthless regimes unafraid to use violent pressure against the wealthy nations which, for their part, can be expected to grab the disappearing resources by force.

MEDICINE AND THE SICK SOCIETY

Population growth is a product not simply of poverty but also of modern science. The aim of medicine is to save and prolong life regardless of the prevailing conditions. Rather than opting for the cynical solution of neglecting to save life, the answer is to improve living conditions. But industrialization itself has an adverse effect on conditions and nowhere more than in its headquarters, the big cities. Even so, most of the development aid of the wealthy countries has gone to the cities. Several developing nations, where the only hope of independent progress lies in developing agriculture around the villages, are being supplied with atomic energy installations in order to accelerate the rate of industrialization. Population growth leads to increasing pressure on the diminishing and over-farmed agricultural areas and to migration into the cities. In 25 years there may be cities of 50 million inhabitants, the vast majority of whom will be packed together in conditions defying anything we can imagine today.

Even in the wealthy countries we have not managed to make the urban environment healthy. Medicine may have succeeded in combatting and virtually eradicating those diseases which once claimed the greatest number of victims, but at the same time other

31

diseases have become more common. According to the latest U.N. report 40% of all cases of cancer in industrial societies are believed to be due to environmental causes. It is not merely a range of preservative, colorant and other synthetic substances that are pathogenic, however, but also a range of medical drugs. The impressive results of medicine have proved an ideal means of strengthening belief in development, up to a point. Ivan Illich, who has cast doubt in several books on the efficacy of large institutions within the health and education services, speaks of two watersheds in medicine. The first of these was around 1913 when patients began to have a more than 50-50 chance of effective treatment, when the infant mortality rate fell and when average life expectancy rose sharply. The second came around 1955, after which 'preservation of the sick life of medically dependent people in an unhealthy environment became the principal business of the medical profession' (*Tools for Conviviality*, p.3). This view may not be totally fair to the medical profession, but it is a fact that industrial society invests far more in curative than in preventive medicine and that the growth in medical services has not decreased the numbers of diseases or diseased lives. According to W.H.O. figures 70% of health service expenditure in the cities is used for treating patients who die within a year.

Prevention of damage to the environment, or rather improvement of the environment is beyond the scope of a single science; it is a task which demands organized collaboration between various kinds of expert. However, as social problems have become more and more complex, there has been a simultaneous tendency to greater professional specialization, and professional associations appear to be more preoccupied with the economic interests of their members than with the needs of society.

TECHNOLOGY FOR
DESTRUCTION OR CONSTRUCTION?

If even a humanitarian science like medicine can be described as serving to preserve diseased life in an unhealthy environment, what can we say of the purpose served by the other sciences? Since the nuclear physicists made their appeals to the world in the 1950s there has been no lack of warnings from eminent scientists against the misuse of scientific achievements. But against this must be set the facts, first that scientists are always contradicting one another, and second that the specialized knowledge of others makes only a limited impression on people at large. What really matters, in any case, is that nations, business concerns and researchers themselves are constantly spurred on by the necessity of being first in the race.

It is no coincidence that something in the nature of a state of war prevails in this sphere. The enormous economic growth after the Second World War was partly based on the 'second technological revolution' – and behind this lay the Second World War which accelerated research and the application of its results. As the West German Defence Ministry so clearly expressed it, 'the extreme demands on arms technology will automatically result in a challenge to science and technology to produce the highest achievements'. The great technological advances have been made in military and space research and have since been partly used for 'peaceful purposes' as with nuclear power, radar, supersonic civil aircraft. It is possible to trace a specific development pattern for these areas of technology: state-financed basic research and product development in collaboration between the public sector and advanced industrial companies – involving such huge investment that it is difficult to discontinue the product even if it proves to be of little use and to make a considerable financial loss. The supersonic civil aircraft is an example of this; it is also an example of the significant part played by nationalistic motives in the race to be first. Demands have been made in France that no planes from New York should land in Paris unless the Anglo-French supersonic aircraft were allowed to land in New York.

We may have continuous disarmament negotiations but they do not lead to arms limitation, and could thus be seen as an attempt to baffle the enemy, i.e. the public. In any case, despite these talks, there are still more people employed in the development of new weaponry than in any other branch of research: 400,000 scientists and engineers are engaged in military research and development programmes which account for 40% of the entire expenditure on research programmes. Although the superpowers have the capacity to annihilate each other fifty times over, development still continues of new weapons more overwhelming in their destructive force than anything hitherto known. (A recent triumph of the researchers is the neutron bomb which can kill people by radiation and leave material goods intact).

Just as armaments like these are described as deterrents and defensive weapons, despite the fact that research programmes concentrate on offensive weapons, so the arms industry is frequently regarded as a driving force for economic development, even though it goes without saying that the vast sums invested in military equipment could be better used for civilian purposes or to combat poverty and hardship in the world. It is the driving force in an insane form of development that leads mankind further and further away from any possible solution to its common problems. The only group to benefit from this area of development is the arms industry which works so closely with the state (both in the U.S. and elsewhere) that leading politicians are more likely to help than to hinder it. The arms trade is particularly profitable, and the Third World is a particularly good market; in many developing countries there are military regimes, or military forces threatening the regime which must be pacified with military equipment. The American arms trade with its central administration in the Pentagon controls almost half the market, but neutral countries like Sweden and Switzerland are also large exporters of arms and therefore specifically committed to military research.

Since the state is deeply implicated in the arms industry throughout the world nationalization will make no appreciable difference. To see how little the well-meaning politician can do, we have only to look to President Eisenhower's warning against the military-industrial complex and Premier Khrushchev's admission in conversation with him that he had the same problem. Even with state ownership of the production sector the Soviet Union has not succeeded in developing a technology any different from that in the capitalist countries; there, too, the arms industry is more extensive than any other.

While military research is often justified on the grounds that it can be harnessed to peaceful ends, branches of research that are justified on the grounds that they do serve the cause of mankind can be used for other purposes. This is particularly true of molecular biology which may produce an unprecedented control

34

over nature by transferring genetic characteristics from one species of plant or animal to another. It is said to be possible, for example, to fabricate new strains of cereal that do not require fertilizer, bacteria that produce insulin, organisms able to absorb oil spillage – and better kept away from oil pipelines. The greatest risk lies in the possibility of the manipulated coli bacillus especially used for such experiments turning out to have unforeseen properties and thus causing new epidemic diseases. In most countries, there are commissions to supervise developments in this field; but there can be no doubt that those in power will make use of whatever means they can and that research will supply the means. Either society must adapt to suit people's needs or people must adapt to suit the needs of society, and this second alternative might well come about as a result of genetic engineering and concealed technological control of behaviour. Anyone believing that technological development will solve all our problems must look ahead to solutions like these. In fact the problems are created to a large extent by technical development itself.

The example we have quoted from molecular biology raises the whole question of whether the traditional freedom accorded to basic research can be maintained. This freedom is particularly problematic in a social system where the production sector (under cover of the right to commercial secrecy) uses the results of research to develop new technology motivated by narrow economic criteria – and where the control exercised by society is weak and imposed after the event. Freedom of research would be less dangerous if technological development of this kind were subordinate to human considerations, or in other words if it were brought under democratic control. It is not technology itself that is the trouble but the alliance between 'disinterested' research (which does not care about how its results are exploited) and economic and power-political interests. Technology can only become constructive rather than destructive when it is serving policies that are economic in the true sense of the word, i.e. careful with resources. What we should be asking is not how much can be produced and how much profit the product will make, but what ought to be produced and what use it will serve. But before this question can be answered in practice both economic and political systems must undergo radical changes.

THE ECONOMY IS NOT ECONOMICAL

The economy of modern industrialized societies is not based on economization, either in theory or in practice, but on ever-increasing growth. Just as the instruments of destruction form a crucial part of production and an essential source of the profit that drives development further along the wrong road, so does the huge waste involved in capitalist means of production appear on the positive side when it comes to calculating the gross national product. Traffic accidents, for example, cause considerable human and economic loss to society, and yet they figure on the plus side of the national balance sheet because they give rise to 'productive' work in the forms of repairs, medical services and so on. Despite every conceivable scientific and technical advance the social balance sheet is still so primitive that it does not give any real account of how economically natural and human resources are used.

The rule that governs individual enterprises, namely that it is bad economics to live off capital, does not govern human enterprise as a whole, if we take 'capital' to be natural resources. One of the main reasons for this is that individual enterprises, which cannot afford to run at a loss year after year (as society as a whole can do), can afford to leave the external problems to society. This necessitates organized control on the part of society and an expanding bureaucracy, though it would be a more economical solution to change the aims and objectives of business so that they coincided with those of society.

One of the features of capitalist production methods is the abundance of private decision-making bodies which have the freedom to produce what they choose and to use their profits as they wish – and which are primarily devoted to creating profits. Another feature is the competition between companies – not to be first to satisfy real needs but to win the race to exploit new technological opportunities. The result of this is that resources are being squandered at an ever-accelerating rate; both products and manufacturing machinery become obsolete before the end of their useful life. Economic life time is shorter than technical life time. It does not pay, therefore, to make products as durable as possible: waste becomes economical.

Seen in this light, the statement that 'what is good for the big companies is good for society' begins to sound somewhat unconvincing. Indeed, it is clear that what is rational and economical for the big company may well be uneconomical and irrational for society. Given its specific aims, the business enterprise is almost duty bound *not* to give maximum consideration to the environment. The discrepancy between private and public sector interests becomes particularly serious when business takes risks with inadequate safety measures in order to cut costs. The Seveso poisoning disaster in 1976 is a particularly grave example of such practices, but it is not the only one. The rule is that economic considerations take precedence over considerations of safety; the fact that production methods can be kept secret on grounds of competition makes it difficult for the public to maintain adequate control. Indeed, local or regional authorities often go out of their way to attract businesses which might stimulate economic development in their area.

An economic system which is based *primarily* on efficient production in an atmosphere of stiff competition cannot make its *primary* objectives the creation of full employment, the protection of employees' welfare or the satisfaction of their need for meaningful work – as emerges clearly enough from the fact that many working environments, even within the welfare state, are frustrating or damaging to health. Company accounting systems reckon human labour alongside other production factors like raw materials and machinery. The traditional way of increasing profits is to keep wages down, though the strength of the unions and even the democratic ideology of equality have made this increasingly difficult. The importation of foreign labour may reduce wages but society has to carry the expense of educating the workers and their families and the social problems that inevitably occur when a group of people is introduced into a foreign community. In most European countries the importation of foreign labour during a boom period has given rise to increased problems during the subsequent recession, when the trend to reduce human labour becomes more acute. 'It is thought-provoking and symptomatic,' writes Karl Henrik Pettersson in his book *Reap the Whirlwind* (p.106), 'that of the gross investments of developed countries some 60-70% are devoted to rationalization and new forms of technology for increasing efficiency, the ultimate aim of which is to replace labour by capital'. When business 'rationalizes away' the labour force, society must again carry the economic burden in the form of unemployment benefits, retraining costs, etc.

It is of course possible, in theory at any rate, to combat this trend from within the economic system. Modern management theory has made it plain that performance deteriorates when the working environment is bad and that greater influence over one's own working conditions increases efficiency, but there is little evidence of these perceptions being put into practice. Nor has the liberalistic belief that ownership provides an incentive for supreme effort been reflected in any endeavour to secure co-ownership for employees in general.

According to some of the modern liberal economists it is also possible to include the so-called externalities in the company balance sheet, though business has seldom made any active effort to do so. Besides, the question still remains whether it is in fact possible to measure and account for damage to health and environment. How high a price should we put on the absence of bird song, on the adverse effects of soil drainage on fish life, or on the damage done to the landscape by a high voltage line? How should we evaluate economic remuneration for chronic ill-health or loss of life caused by efficient production? How is economic compensation supposed to make up for such losses? The fact that it is technically possible to include externalities of this kind on the economic balance sheet does not solve any problems.

The case is the same for damage caused to the environment by the common use of manufactured products. How are we to construct a reasonable bill for the proportion of total air pollution caused by an individual car-owner or cigarette-smoker? It would be an impossible and futile enterprise, just as it would be no solution to make access to healthy natural surroundings dependent on individual wealth.

ECONOMIC FREEDOM, EQUALITY AND THE RIGHT OF OWNERSHIP

It is an old liberal dogma that it is the consumer who ultimately decides what is going to be produced. In theory the market mechanism ensures that there will be a proper balance between supply and demand. When demand for a product exceeds supply the price rises and the least interested parties cease to purchase. When supply exceeds demand the price falls; if the product still fails to attract enough buyers then production must be cut or halted altogether. In this way the wishes of the consumer will control production by way of the market mechanism.

In practice things work out quite differently. The consumers who are the first to stop buying when prices rise are not those who have least need for the product but those who can least afford it. In a society dominated by economic inequality the market mechanism ensures that the well-to-do are the last to give up the scarce goods. According to its theory, or rather according to the ideas of the earliest liberal economists, the market mechanism can only function fairly in a society where there is economic equality.

Something similar applies to the other governing principle of the liberal economists: free competition. In theory this ensures that the nation does not waste its resources on inefficient production methods, since the more efficient producer eliminates its less efficient competitors: only healthy companies survive. However, free competition will only be economical for society as long as the losers can be put to use in other areas of production (and do not require social support), and competition will only be free as long as the companies involved are roughly the same size, as they were in the time of Adam Smith when the theory was new and sensational. Free competition results in the well-known principle that 'to him who hath shall be given . . .' Competition will, so to speak, outcompete freedom.

Paradoxically, the equitable use of both free competition and the market mechanism seems to be conditional on: (1) restricting economic freedom of action, and (2) achieving economic equality.

To start with point 1, it is of course true that economic freedom of action *has* been restricted since the days when early liberalism was new. Anti-trust legislation, employer liability, public institutions to protect the environment, unions, consumer organizations, regulations concerning prices and profits etc. are all evidence of this. But 'almost without exception the regulations are concerned with spheres other than the area of production in which the firm is engaged . . . On the whole, companies in a capitalist system are still free to make whatever they please . . .

the forces of the free market have been limited and balanced in virtually all areas except the one which could justifiably be considered the most important' (*Reap the Whirlwind*, p.126). The question remains as to whether restrictions in the most important area will not make many other restrictions superfluous. The problem is that the alternative to a 'free' economy (i.e. the freedom of business to produce anything it wants) is an economy controlled by society, and this is usually associated with a sluggish and uneconomical bureaucracy.

Against arguments that the public sector impedes productive business with its red tape, must be raised the point that the public sector has grown mainly in order to stimulate the economy and to remedy the uneconomic effects of the economic system. The basic reason for the growth in bureaucracy is the built-in conflict of interests within the social system, and the chief reason for *this* is freedom of economic action for the private sector. A system of this kind requires more and more regulations and control, a larger administration and so on.

The question of social control of production also calls into question the right to private ownership of the means of production, which sometimes emerges from liberal tradition as the major democratic right, although a right which is reserved for a tiny minority can hardly be described as democratic. On this point it is sufficient to refer to E. F. Schumacher's reasoning:

(*a*) In small-scale enterprise, private ownership is natural, fruitful and just.

(*b*) In medium-scale enterprise, private ownership is already to a large extent functionally unnecessary. The idea of 'property' becomes strained, unfruitful and unjust. If there is only one owner or a small group of owners, there can be, and should be, a voluntary surrender of privilege to the wider group of actual workers . . .

(*c*) In large-scale enterprise, private ownership is a fiction for the purpose of enabling functionless owners to live parasitically on the labour of others. It is not only unjust but also an irrational element which distorts all relationships within the enterprise (*Small is Beautiful*, p. 223).

The same line of argument can be used against the absurd private ownership of others' housing and of the world's resources.

Private ownership is frequently defended by reference to the situation in socialist countries where the two-fold bureaucracy of party and state has been unable either to satisfy the citizens' demands for consumer goods or to establish economic parity, let alone other civil rights. However, there is a difference between social control of production and joint state and party control of the whole of economic and political life. It is, of course, no coincidence that there is no freedom of consumer choice where there is no freedom of political choice; nor is it coincidence that the relative autonomy of business ventures in Yugoslavia is apparently dependent on a relatively free market.

For historic reasons the market mechanism has been linked to the capitalist society with its economic inequalities, although it could only in fact function fairly in a society characterized by economic equality. Leaving aside those goods and services vital for specific social groups, such as the sick and handicapped, the market mechanism provides a simple and unbureaucratic system of distribution. Furthermore, assuming that production is oriented towards the satisfaction of real needs and that the citizens are on the same economic footing, it will not produce anti-social repercussions or social imbalance. When economic equality prevails it is possible to tax consumption rather than labour – and to abolish income tax and a large part of the bureaucracy with it.

Going on to point 2: just as constraints are imposed upon economic freedom for social reasons, so should economic inequality be narrowed down for democratic reasons. Standardization of income does more to further economic equality than an uneven distribution of wealth followed by counteractive measures in the form of graduated taxation and various subsidies and allowances, many of which achieve the opposite effect. During the affluent 1960s the gap between the highest and lowest incomes remained the same; in a situation where there was more for everybody inequalities gave rise to less discontent than they have done in the less affluent 1970s. Although efforts are made to keep pace with inflation through index-linking, the distribution of wealth is as one-sided as ever. In Denmark, for example 3% of the population in 1975 owned over one quarter of the private

41

capital, 11% owned over half.

There is no evidence that economic growth leads to a fairer distribution of wealth. But economic equalization is one of the crucial preconditions for restricting the growth in material consumption both nationally and internationally.

Attempts have been made to justify inequality in liberalist theory: offering the highest rewards to the most important functions in society will summon up the most outstanding ability and qualifications to the benefit of all. From this it may be supposed that restricting economic freedom will paralyze initiative and lead to a sluggish economic and social life. The mythical hero of capitalism is the paperboy, bellhop or shoeshine boy who winds up a multi-millionaire and president of a vast business empire. Closer analysis of such businessmen will probably reveal, however, that their chief quality was a special talent for exploiting the rules of society to the utmost (and a little further), for buying land and property at the right time, for buying cheap and selling at a profit. This is very much in the spirit of the system but not to the advantage of society. The earth could have been exploited quite enough without land speculators; there could have been enough houses without property speculators. Obviously constraints on economic freedom may act as a brake on the most speculative commercial ventures, but most people will not suffer as a result.

In a society where levels of education are high, people with professional qualifications and management ability are not rarities to be courted; indeed most of those people who have made original contributions to the fields of research, technology and the arts are not motivated by the desire for economic gain. There is a great deal of evidence that the greed for wealth is more a psychological disorder caused by the social environment than an original human driving force – there may well be a hint of this too in the capitalist myth we have already mentioned about the least in society who becomes the greatest.

THE BIG COMPANIES AND THE TECHNOSTRUCTURE

Of course it is not the ordinary consumers that demand supersonic flight, nuclear power plants and vast hospitals. In many cases there are protests against them from the citizens whose lives are affected by projects like these (sometimes objections are raised to the siting of a motorway through a specific part of town even though the local residents make frequent use of other motorways). As far as ordinary consumer goods are concerned, freedom of consumer choice is also more restricted in practice than in theory. Mass production in the big firms is not regulated mainly by consumer desires; if anything it is the consumer who has his desires regulated.

J. K. Galbraith in particular has emphasized this and has exposed the myth of consumer sovereignty. He distinguishes between two sectors in the economy: the market system which includes smaller firms and farms, small independent craftsmen etc., and the planning system dominated by big firms which control an ever greater part of an increasingly restricted market. In 1968 the 200 largest corporations in the U.S.A. controlled the same percentage (around 65%) of all assets employed in manufacturing as the 1000 largest had done in 1941. The following features are characteristic of the big firms:

1. They operate in many areas of production and most of them work in many countries; this is why they are commonly known as multi-nationals, although the vast majority of them are American.
2. Their production is based on advanced technology, basic research and product development. This necessitates such enormous long-term investment that the companies are bound to ensure that their products will sell by use of market research, marketing, advertising and sometimes even corruption.
3. They are not managed by the owners, the shareholders, but by an 'association of men of diverse technical knowledge, experience or other talent which modern industrial technology and planning require' (*The New Industrial State*, p.59). This is the 'technostructure'. The technostructure is less interested in maximising profits for the owners than in expanding the company to the benefit of themselves and the other employees; investment in automation equipment is not necessarily undertaken with a view to reducing costs, the real reason may be a desire for increased power and security for the management (less trouble with the labour force).

4. They often operate in concert with the state, which in many cases – and particularly in the military industrial sector – is the companies' biggest customer. Heads of state sometimes appear to be acting as representatives for the firms (as did Nixon for Lockheed). The big companies are able to exercise a powerful influence on the foreign policy of the state; this is especially true of the U.S.A., as shown by I.T.T. in Chile and the oil companies in the Middle East.

Galbraith has pointed out the discrepancy between liberalist theory and the actual situation in industry; theoretically the American competitive enterprise is an acknowledged profit and loss system, but in reality the losses are suffered by the market system while society cannot tolerate the prospect of competition leading to failure for the big firms. The traditional American fear of state domination over economic life is one reason why economic life has come to dominate the state; public bodies set up to control the companies are beginning to look more like hostages than controllers. The technostructure is becoming a vast, anonymous power factor which can use its ability to influence the market and the public sector bureaucracy to promote particular development trends in modern society. A few top managers in a big concern can make decisions that will affect the employment, income and geographical location of countless people.

The biggest companies, which are economically greater than minor states like Denmark, can make it difficult for nation states to conduct an independent economic policy. They can evade labour legislation and tax policies in one country by transferring production or profits to the most accommodating nations; in the developing countries they frequently contribute to maladjusted technological and social development in order to keep corrupt regimes in power. The big companies thus form a considerable barrier to the expansion of democracy. Only the technostructure can cope with the heavy demands for research and development in areas of expensive technology; the engineers need little urging to rush into the development of new and exciting technologies. As a rule the professional challenge will outweigh any scruples about social consequences.

In his analysis of the big company planning system, which persuades the consumer to buy many unnecessary goods,

Galbraith has emphasized that the system pulls the wool over the public's eyes, and that greater insight into the real economic facts could threaten the companies; but the general public find it easier to identify with private than with public interests. There are, however, signs of a change in attitude: opinion polls conducted in 1976 showed that only 20% of American citizens had any confidence in big business. In the present era of 'late capitalism' with its diminishing supply of capital and its falling returns on investment (one reason for the big companies' move into further new areas of production), the big firms will in fact be more vulnerable than the small ones and their need for expansion makes it difficult for them to readjust to a more socially useful economy. There are, therefore, not merely democratic but also economic reasons for fighting against the power concentrated in the technostructure of the big firms.

Despite the many resources of the technostructure it also has a number of built-in weaknesses. Generally speaking coordination between different branches within the technostructure is not good, and the market does not function efficiently when it is dealing with specialized demands for raw materials, components and labour. Here the long delays inherent in the system may lead to awkward economic cycles. Galbraith maintains quite simply that the technostructure is fundamentally unstable and can only hold its own with support from the public sector bureaucracy. As a result it is possible that present developments will be modified to the benefit of smaller firms, a trend which can already be traced within certain sectors of business.

INTERNATIONALIZATION OF THE ECONOMY

Since the end of the Second World War there has been steadily increasing economic integration between the Western industrial countries, as regards both international trade and international investments. Leaving aside isolated cases of monopoly in raw materials (such as the O.P.E.C. countries), there can be little doubt that international trade imposes fewer constraints on national freedom of action than international investment. Increasing markets lead to a wider choice of importing and exporting countries for most goods. On the other hand, it becomes difficult for a nation to conduct an independent

45

economic policy if a significant part of its production capital is owned or controlled by foreign companies. In this context, therefore, there are good reasons for paying more attention to international investments than to trade.

As a general rule international trade figures are easily accessible, while it is much more difficult to obtain information about investment figures. One of the official justifications for this is the need for discretion about industrial data which could be abused by competitors. There is therefore scant evidence on which to base scientific research in this field. Most analyses concentrate on the economic consequences of more widespread international division of production; the political repercussions have not been subjected to similar scrutiny.

Early liberal theories about international division of production and trade were based on geographical variations in climate, mineral deposits, population structure etc. Subsequent development, however, has not supported this line of reasoning; it is obvious that the major international trade today takes place between industrial nations of roughly similar structure. This also applies to international investment. We must therefore look for other causes than those mentioned above. As far as small countries in particular are concerned, it is worth mentioning the necessity of going beyond the narrow domestic market with specialized products in areas of advanced technology.

In the last decade it has become more common to supplement or substitute traditional foreign trade with the establishment of manufacturing plants abroad. This enables the company to avoid customs duty, to reduce transport costs, to take advantage of cheap labour, to distribute the risks, to ensure supplies of raw materials and to obtain technical know-how and marketing information by buying up foreign companies. Finally there may be political motives associated with a desire to propagate the capitalist system, particularly in the developing nations. Foreign production can thus be advantageous to the individual firm; whether there is any real advantage in terms of the use of world resources is more difficult to determine, just as it is harder to pinpoint the consequences for individual countries. There is much to suggest, however, that international investment has been most beneficial to the (large) rich nations.

In 1976 Svante Iger published a report on the internationalization of the Swedish economy. This document demonstrates that foreign investment in Sweden has gone chiefly into the purchase of companies involved in advanced technology, 'future-oriented' production (i.e. the chemical, electronics and machine tool industries).

It is a feature of development in Sweden that internationalization and the concentration of finance have gone hand in hand. The ten largest foreign companies operating in Sweden are all multinational corporations, (Philips, I.T.T., I.B.M., Siemens, Unilever, etc.). However, the influence and the financial concentration of the big companies is very selective and product-oriented. To use the Swedish experience as an example, the four largest firms there account for 98% of all margarine products; in other parts of the food industry (mustard, icecream, soup, etc.) the corresponding percentage is between 90 and 100%. The four largest companies control 79% of the market in detergents and 100% of the market in car tyres.

Despite this trend, only 6.5% of total sales of Swedish manufactured products in 1972 came from foreign subsidiaries, and in 1974 there were three times as many people employed in Swedish owned subsidiaries abroad as in foreign owned subsidiary companies in Sweden. Of the 1200 foreign subsidiaries in Sweden only one quarter were involved in industrial production, the rest exclusively in sales and service.

The Swedish pattern shows that foreign trade has grown much stronger than international investment. In 1974 Swedish exports and imports corresponded to roughly one third of the gross national product; the nine largest exporting companies were responsible for one third of Swedish exports, the 22 largest for one half.

It has thus been possible for a small country like Sweden to establish material living standards among the highest in the world by active participation in international trade, without relying to any great extent on foreign capital invested in domestic manufacture. There is, however, no certainty that it will be possible to maintain this position in the longer term. The need for ever increasing investment in industrial research and development may force countries like Sweden to abandon aspirations of independent achievements in many fields of advanced technology.

INTERNATIONAL CONSTRAINTS ON FREEDOM OF ACTION: THE CASE OF DENMARK

Danish exports today also constitute roughly one third of the gross national product, and foreign trade is crucially important for the Danish economy. What effect does this have on Danish political freedom of action? Could Denmark, for example, seek to become a low-energy society or to introduce co-ownership for employees in Danish firms independently of its E.E.C. partners? The answers to these questions are looking more positive than might immediately be expected. The more extensive collaboration within the E.E.C. becomes, the harder it will obviously be to conduct a policy that is not in accord with that of the other member nations. On the other hand, there is a tendency to exaggerate these constraints, perhaps a very conscious tendency; those who regard economic integration as an end in itself will also invoke the need for standardized political evolution.

The flight of capital is one of the terrors conjured up whenever it is suggested that changes might be made in the ownership and decision-making structures within the production sector. It is not, of course, inconceivable that some capitalists would seek to transfer their assets to another country if they found that Denmark was following a less 'pro-capitalist' course than other Western industrial nations. But such transfers of capital are not easy to effect; firstly the company has to be sold, and secondly permission must be obtained from the National Bank to transfer large amounts of money abroad. Society already has the necessary means to control this process. Up to a certain point ways may always be found to make illegal monetary transfers but these are hardly likely to disrupt the balance of the economy; and if needed society will be able to take countermeasures against this kind of economic sabotage.

As we have seen from the Swedish example, it is not essential to attract more foreign companies in order to raise material living standards. What is essential is an industry that is competitive in the export market and that can compete with imports at home. Given that, the nation will be a reliable and viable trading partner, relatively independent of its political line.

In what ways can Danish industry adapt to international

development? There are suggestions that even comparatively strong industrial countries like Sweden must expect to find themselves lagging behind in many areas of advanced technology because of their limited size. Instead of trying to be miniature copies of the large industrial nations the smaller nations ought rather to conduct an alternative industrial policy. Danish industry has already made a move in this direction; partly voluntarily it has abandoned hopes of being counted among the producers of aircraft, nuclear energy installations, large computers and even cars. Danish firms are very small by world standards and are not generally capable of mass production on a large scale. To a certain extent accusations that the nation has a smallholder mentality are justified. But this attitude can be used to advantage in efforts to create specialized, high-quality products and advanced 'intermediate technology' designed for small units; in many fields smaller firms will be more flexible than the big companies.

Another obvious area in which Denmark could evolve a more independent policy is agriculture. Since the rise in affluence began in the early 1960s, food production in Denmark has stagnated while it has advanced in other European countries, apart from Portugal. There have been increasing encroachments on agricultural land in order to build luxury houses, holiday homes, hotels, roads, supermarkets, parking lots, etc. At the same time the price of land and agricultural property has risen so that young people have found it excessively difficult to take over farms and must work excessively hard to make them profitable. A report on agriculture issued in the spring of 1977 recommended an annual increase of 3% in livestock production as the figure to aim for. Considering the world shortage of foodstuffs, and in particular of protein, it is doubtful whether this is the right product area on which to concentrate. It takes more protein to produce one kilogram of beef than the beef itself contains, and it is not clear that a vast production and exportation of livestock will help to increase world food supplies. At the same time, there is a greater need for healthy food, although there has been no general move to institute research into ecological agriculture which is both less dependent on artificial fertilizers and crop sprays and less energy consuming. In this field agricultural countries like Denmark could break new ground, with particular emphasis on the production of healthy vegetable products.

There is a great deal of evidence that international division of labour when carried too far will make the world system more unstable. Failures and difficulties in one part of the system will affect every related area. Market fluctuations spread unerringly to all the industrialized countries. If individual regions were to become more self-supporting, particularly in basic areas such as food, energy, etc. then the world would undoubtedly gain. This may be difficult for a single nation to achieve but is quite possible for many groups of neighbouring nations with close cultural and political relations. Scandinavia *could* be an example.

It is not only in Denmark that doubts are being raised about the efficacy of the traditional economic system. If the Danes attempted to use their influence in order to direct future development towards an ecologically sustainable society, their working partners would not necessarily try to block the idea. It has been known for small countries to act as pioneers, as they did with the development of the welfare state.

THE NATIONAL ECONOMY

Lack of raw materials makes countries like Denmark particularly sensitive to international trade conditions. No economic depression, however, has forced them for decades to use more than they produce and to finance their trade deficits with foreign loans. This actually means that they make no contribution to offsetting hardship in the world, a fact which is particularly shameful because very little sacrifice would be required to change the situation. The obstacle to change is the conflict of interests within society which was concealed by the rise of affluence in the 1960s but which has re-emerged during the recession of the 1970s.

Since over-consumption is synonymous with trade deficits, the simple solution is to limit imports and increase exports (a natural step to take when there is high unemployment). But a European country like Denmark cannot presume to impose import restrictions because of its membership of the E.E.C. and other international organizations. Besides, trade restrictions lead to similar measures being taken in other countries and to more acute crises (there is an incipient move in this direction already:

the E.E.C. has imposed restrictions on textile imports from a number of developing countries, the U.S.A. has restricted shoe imports from Taiwan and Korea, etc.). There are limits to the liberalism of the large countries when their own industry is not sufficiently competitive. The French president Giscard d'Estaing talks of 'organized free trade'!).

Far from being able to solve both unemployment and balance of payments problems simultaneously, efforts to ease one problem result in exacerbation of the other. The traditional political means of creating more jobs is to step up consumption within the confines of the home market. But consumers do not differentiate clearly between domestic and foreign products, they look at the price. Increased consumption leads to correspondingly greater consumption of imported goods, to higher employment abroad and to greater trade deficits. The traditional means of reducing the trade deficit is to restrict consumption by increased taxes on goods and services. In Denmark there was a political settlement in September 1975 aimed specifically at increasing consumption, and another in August 1976 aimed specifically at limiting it. Neither of them helped solve these problems.

Taking a long term view, and a not so very long term if it comes to that, the great problem lies both in too large a consumption and in uncontrolled production. At a time when economic growth *has* been halted by a depression, circumstances should be more favourable for policies which accept that growth must be halted. The time must surely have come for us to recognize that the greatest possible demand and the greatest possible supply have no intrinsic value. From the point of view of world resources and social economy, it is better that half as many people should be employed producing healthy products and more durable goods, than that twice as many should be employed producing twice as many products which are only half as good. However, this argument has had no success in the face of world unemployment which nations everywhere are attempting to solve by short-sighted and traditional means – and with the same poor results. For it is at times of crisis that longsighted measures are postponed until better days; and this despite the fact that when the good times do come there is no incentive to change anything, as we know full well, and despite the fact that short term measures only serve to defer the problems and make the long term measures that much more difficult.

Several economists have recognized that we cannot produce our way out of unemployment. If productivity is increased at a faster rate than markets, things are going wrong; and if conservative politicians were to succeed in imposing their demands for job-cutting in the public sector, things would go wrong even more quickly. At the moment 'the right to work' is a symbolic statement of intent that can only be put into practice if there is a radical change of employment principles in the labour market and an improved distribution of socially useful work. The unemployment problem cannot be solved by traditional means, and it is to a large extent caused by those trends which need to be changed. To round off the argument we need only point out that there is a connection between growth and inflation. The idea that consumption pays now while saving does not pay at all is further reinforced by an economic policy that encourages borrowing. This strengthens the pressure for higher wages and weakens confidence in the economic policy.

Marxists are well aware that the fiercer competition of 'late capitalism' goes hand in hand with falling profit margins, but they appear nonetheless ready to focus their criticism on the fat profits of the capitalists. It is a fact that wages have increased more in Denmark over the past few years than in most other countries and that the wages bill accounts for an ever-increasing proportion of production costs, while profit has been falling (the large profits made by some firms do not alter the general picture). The wage bill cannot rise much higher without even more firms going bankrupt.

The pressure on wages reinforces the trend towards rationalization and automation; fear of unemployment can be used as pressure to achieve greater productivity, which further reduces the need for labour; productivity deals are accepted by the workers' unions because those who are actually in work gain in the short term, although deals of this kind are more deleterious to workers and reduce the need for labour.

In 1977 the largest newspaper publishers in Denmark suffered a crisis which bore several features characteristic of the crisis of capitalism. To begin with the firm offers higher wages, not just to increase productivity but also as a means of competing against other publishers; costs rise more sharply than income; labour-saving machinery is introduced; workers are fired; the workers fight more for jobs in general than for their specific job; a union secretary states that the firm will have to close if demands are not met, although this will mean unemployment for hundreds of people who happen to be members of other unions. 'It has nothing to do with the money' comes the assertion, but this statement does not mean that any one group in society is pre-pared to give up the least part of its cash so that others may have a job. The different groups look after their own interests at the expense of others, and with such lack of foresight that they may even on occasion be in conflict with their own interests.

The oil drivers' strike which almost paralyzed Denmark in the spring of 1976 emphasized how absurd it is that the most socially necessary work should be amongst the lower paid. However, the strike as a weapon is not reserved for the low paid in their struggle against capitalism; it has also become a conventional weapon of blackmail against society for any strong union whose members are not in fact suffering hardship – and whose self-interest is a substantial barrier to fair government and to the solving of economic problems.

The social-democrats' slogan for May 1 1977 was 'Join the fight against self-interest'. Nevertheless, in the same year the leader of the Danish Trades Union Congress stated, 'This is how we all keep going, and if we fail to nurse it along and to ensure that people do get the chance to develop because of their self-interest, everything will grind to a halt'. This statement is an admission of the good old liberal belief in self-interest as the driving force in society. Modern society furnishes an object lesson in the anti-social effects of this belief. On the same occasion the union leader also observed that the kind of economic democracy which gives workers a share in ownership and profits 'cements the system of private capitalism' which he apparently found acceptable.

It may of course be necessary, if not to nurse self-interest along, then at least to treat the kind of self-interest that begrudges others getting more than oneself (in a word, envy), as an established socio-psychological reality in modern society. It is a phenomenon which cannot be removed by appeals to morality but only by the removal of its basic cause, economic inequality. A fair distribu-tion of wealth is the first pre-requisite for a halt to the wages spiral and for preventing strategically placed groups from crippling society with strikes on the grounds that other groups receive higher wages.

The introduction of equal wages will gradually deprive the unions of their right to negotiate wage settlements for their members and thus remove their present extra-parliamentary influence on the economy. In principle, it must be up to the government and parliament to decide wage levels; the right of free negotiation between organizations has proved to be an illusion, although union power is still great enough to make the government's power over the economy an illusion too.

It is doubtful whether the union leader quoted above was right in saying that the system of private capitalism as it has existed until now is acceptable. We do not intend to discuss here whether the capitalist system will inevitably collapse; but it is certain that it has not been able to avoid regular crises, that the big problems cannot be solved within the framework of the system, and that the more serious the crisis the more restricted freedom of action becomes. Ever sharper conflicts will lead to a collapse, and then such dictatorial measures will be called for that it will be hard for democracy to survive. In a rich society it is not thought to be progressive politics to work for polarization and confrontation – it is more sensible to bear in mind that 'at a certain level the question of power over the means of production becomes more important than the sharing of the national income' (*Mandel*) – not so much a question of earning more as of more participation.

One of the basic objections to a change in direction is that a country instituting social and economic experiments is bound to become less creditworthy: our trade deficit restricts our freedom of action. This argues *against* sudden changes that will provoke reactions from outside and *for* a long-term reformist policy in which the settlement of foreign debts plays an important part.

ORGANIZATIONS AND PRESSURE GROUPS

A political move which aims to curb 'self-interest', i.e. to abolish economic motives as the driving force in society, will encounter opposition from the self-interest of organizations and pressure groups.

There can be no doubt that the largest of such organizations have a greater influence over the national economy than even the larger political parties, and unlike the political parties they generally have a monopoly in their own field. Most citizens are attached to one or more organizations which look after their economic interests. Only very few are members of political parties and most of the parties are less representative of particular interests than when they first came into being. Nor is the link between specific organizations and parties as close as it was in the days when these groups were more capable of restricting the activities of the parties. When it comes to negotiations, organizational representatives can take up a much stronger position than the politicians and civil-servants on the opposite side of the table, simply because they can concentrate on the interests of their members and do not need to consider the total economy. In this respect economic pressure groups scarcely differ from private firms. They represent specialized knowledge in their own spheres, so that their combination of professional considerations and economic interests may baffle and confuse their opponents, not to mention the wider public. Organizations play a part in both the drafting and the realization of laws; by this means government and administration avoid the possibility of conflict over political decisions to which the organizations may be opposed. In order to consolidate their own position, organizational leaders must achieve results that will win them prestige in the eyes of their members. The economic strength and authoritarian structure of the large organizations usually result in conservative attitudes and working methods. A close watch is kept on existing membership benefits and attempts are made to gain more along the same lines, especially when it comes to wages. One of the common methods is to seek longer training and thus extra qualifications for organization members, which automatically leads to demands for higher wages. It is worth pointing out that neither society, the consumer nor the politicians demand longer training for social workers, nurses, teachers, etc.; it is the respective organizations that always know what is best for others – and for themselves. As a general rule it is also the organizations that object to any job being done by people who are not qualified but only trained by experience to do it. It is not the local users of small schools and hospitals that want them closed down, nor the employees, but the public authorities and administration in agreement with the organizations. Organization views also carry great weight when it comes to choosing men (and occasionally women) for positions of public responsibility. Organizational men in disguise often get to look after the interests of the public sector in relation to the organizations.

By these means the organizations are able to exercise considerable influence over those sections of society which they wish to see expanded for their own economic reasons – and a great influence over the wages of their own members as well. Negotiations between academic organizations and the state have proved particularly problematic. In this case members of the same organization have found themselves sitting on opposite sides of the negotiating table with none of the conflicts of interest which go some way to dividing the T.U.C. from the Employers Confederation, and with none of the personal motives for insisting on wage limitations which are peculiar to private sector management. This may well be one of the reasons why academics have succeeded in increasing their income in relation to other wage-earning groups who are thereby encouraged to seek increases in their turn. (Wage differentials between the public and private sectors play an important part in wage development.)

In his book *The Ruling Class* the Danish economist Jørgen Dich attempted to demonstrate that institutions within the health, education and welfare sectors have expanded beyond the point at which increased investment produces increased returns, with the result that citizens pay more than they receive: in other words, the growth of institutions is less in the interests of society than in the interests of public sector employees. However, arguments for the necessity of further expansion in these areas are based on consideration for the weaker members of society or on considerations of welfare generally to which it may be difficult to object. Everyone is interested in public services in which they can take a share, but less interested of course in paying for them; and neither the people nor even parliament fully understand the relationship between public services and payment of taxes, especially as the organizational experts who have a great deal of say in legislative commissions are not exactly expert in real social benefits.

It does not improve matters that specific ministers will often make themselves spokesmen for the special interests that fall within the jurisdiction of their own particular ministry. There are any number of reports about ministerial meetings in conflict over savings – in somebody else's department. Anything that is in the general interest but is not championed by a pressure group is neglected to the advantage of special interests.

Jørgen Dich thought that the power exercised by experts and organizations could be combatted by experts in social benefits, i.e. economists who analyze and criticize legislation on the basis of its economic repercussions for society as a whole. There are two arguments against this. First, possible repercussions are not solely economic in nature; and second, specialists in the assessment of economic consequences are surely going to be aware of the economic effect that legislation will have on themselves. This problem can be solved by separating the economic interests of the professionals from their professional interests; once wage differentials are ironed out, the stranglehold of economic self-interest upon social development will weaken.

This will not totally eliminate conflicts of interest; every man wants as much progress in his own area as possible, whether it be a professional field, a local district or other aspects of social life to which he is particularly committed. All these spheres ought therefore to be represented in the political decision-making process, not just behind the scenes but out in the actual political arena.

Compared with techno-economic questions, moral values occupy a very modest position in the political debate. Experts in engineering, law and economics carry most weight in the industrial countries. Despite their moderate numbers these groups have been quite immoderate in their annexation of the politician's real freedom to decide, a fact for which politicians themselves are partly to blame.

Experts are influenced by their professional environment and its special interests; like any other pressure group, they, too, want more power, better working conditions and economic progress. The recognition that there is no such thing as an 'apolitical expert' may pave the way towards a reasonable division of work between experts and politicians. Politicians and citizens need clear, comprehensible information about technical and economic problems; in particular they need to know when technical analyses enter the realms of subjective interpretation and wider

57

social judgement. They must know which facts are being amplified or played down, so that political decisions are not predetermined by the way the experts tailor their reports.

The only way to counteract this is by ensuring that all phases of the experts' work from the formulation of problems to the final report are entirely open and accessible, and by getting experts of differing political affiliations to review the problems. At national policy level, work of this kind could be administered by an assembly which would arrange a comprehensive examination of the important questions and ensure that expert help was equally accessible to both opposition and government.

THE PARTY SYSTEM AND
REPRESENTATIVE DEMOCRACY

The problems of government in modern society are not due solely to the fact that problems have grown more numerous and complex in general, but also to the fact that the tools and means of government have not developed to any great extent. The nation must be governed by laws, and the number of laws continues to grow without government becoming more effective; parliaments are so busy keeping up with development that they have no time to change it.

Less than 10% of the world's population now lives under a form of government than can be described as a parliamentary democracy. If democracy is proving ineffective within this very limited part of the world, there is little hope of a universal conversion to the democratic system. All over the world there is talk of parliaments in crisis; and the growing problems of government result in a lack of confidence in democracy itself, even though the crisis may be primarily due to the fact that the traditional parliamentary systems, rooted as they are in a by-passed historical situation, are not sufficiently democratic.

An important feature of representative democracy is the method by which the representatives are elected and their contact with the electorate. In a dictatorship, candidates for decision-making bodies are nominated from above by the government or the party; the people may be allowed to confirm their 'election'. In a democracy candidates are chosen from below; qualification for election should not depend on obedience to the party, political ambition, organizational interests etc., but on personal and professional qualities known to the electors. Otherwise the voters have no chance of making a personal choice. Democracy must be based on confidence in those who are best qualified, but confidence in candidates who are neither known to nor nominated by the people themselves is bound to be limited.

This raises the question whether it is reasonable that only the political parties are able to nominate candidates and casts doubt upon the present party system as a whole. The proliferation of new parties in the Danish parliament has highlighted both these issues. Their existence is evidence that the old-established parties no longer stand as adequate representatives for a diversity of interests, but it is also evidence that the solution does not lie in the formation of more parties since that makes it even harder to govern.

The Danish consitution ignores the existence of political parties. Paragraph 56 of the constitution reads: 'The members of the Parliament (Folketing) shall be bound solely by their conscience and not by any directions given by their electors'. Nothing is said about not being bound by directions from their party, as they in fact are. And the parties in turn are bound by consideration for the electors, especially the floating voters who have a decisive effect on the distribution of power among the parties. When the parties are fighting for governmental control it is the floating vote they fight for first and foremost. The consequences of this curious fact, namely that it is the voters who are not bound to any one party who achieve special significance in a multi-party system, must surely be to limit the importance of the parties.

Actual selection of candidates now takes place inside the local political organizations. Only a small proportion of the people are members of these party organizations, and only a small proportion of members usually attend nomination meetings. Often the nominated candidates have no connection whatever with the constituency in which they are nominated: in safe seats candidates will be 'elected' by the voters simply because they have been nominated by the party. More votes are cast for the party than for individual candidates (the candidates may quite well be unfamiliar to the electorate), and the candidates who get the most personal votes are always top politicians who have become familiar to most people through television. Televised electioneering is far more influential than local election meetings which only attract a wide public if some leading politician is going to attend. The attention of the electorate is focused on a small number of leading politicians who are found to 'come over' on the TV screen. The fight for votes is more like a race between the party leaders than a debate about the various party manifestoes. The extent to which a political leader can influence the party poll will continue to bolster his or her authority until he or she becomes 'over-exposed' and the party has to cast about for a successor. There are indications that the period of 'safe exposure' is becoming shorter and shorter. And there are good reasons for finding more constructive ways of using television to provide information; its wide possibilities are not being exploited. The main features of the party system can be broken down as follows:

1. Only a few people (nearly all of them men) are spokesmen for the party; authoritarian forms of management make it difficult for independent personalities to assert themselves. A political career depends on loyalty to the leadership.
2. The benefit of the party comes before the benefit of the country, consideration for the party outweighs objective convictions, regard for the electorate is most clearly expressed as fear of losing votes. The chief task of the party is to secure or increase its share of the poll, but since every attempt to change anything in society is unpopular with large groups of voters the party has no power to deal with the major problems. 'It is therefore hazardous to want to solve problems. It is easier to let them remain unsolved,' writes the Danish ex-minister of finance Poul Møller, in his book *Politics from the other Side* (*Politik paa vrangen*); and he quotes as an example the right of the house-owner to have the interest on loans deducted from his taxable income which 'helped to undermine the national economy . . . This resulted in property prices rising sky high to everybody's disadvantage, and was therefore a guarantee that inflation would grow worse.'
3. The decisive negotiations do not take place in parliament but in party rooms or more especially in the Prime Minister's office, and the crucial decisions are not really made by parliament but by the cabinet.
4. Parliament becomes a forum for debates which are designed to

make an impression on the electorate if they are broadcast but which generally have no influence on the final vote which is known in advance. Since the electorate is well aware of this, parliamentary debates are not taken very seriously, but they do weaken the credibility of politicians.

5. Although it is officially a legislative assembly, parliament has to be content with modifying and amending Bills most of which have been introduced by the government, if they are to go any further. The actual Bills are drafted by the central administration and are generally influenced by organizations or civil servants.

6. The rank and file member of parliament has little chance of influencing legislation or even of understanding all its implications. Only the government, which has access to the civil servants in the central administration, receives the necessary expert advice. Committee members have to make themselves into experts of one kind or another, with the result that both they and the relevant minister will be fighting for maximum financial support for their own area of interest without being able to assess the consequences for society as a whole. This reinforces the tendency to make politics a professional career and to prevent the politicians from representing a variety of groups: members of parliament are chiefly recruited from the public service sector.

The present parliamentary *modus operandi* makes it difficult for politicians either to acquire the necessary breadth of vision or to pass it on to the people. The turnout for parliamentary elections indicates that there is a great deal of interest in politics, but between elections, the voters are relegated to the sidelines. The actual interpretation of the term 'representative democracy' poses a problem. Some politicians think that the citizens have handed over total responsibility to them until the time comes to face the electorate's decision at the next election: during the election period it is they who decide how much contact they will have with their constituents. There are politicians who believe that the people should not be bothered by the difficult political problems more than is strictly necessary, and who regard moves from the citizens to influence politicians as incompatible with the basic idea of representative democracy and detrimental to its effectiveness. On the other hand, many citizens feel that they have been deprived of influence over their own affairs, that politicians come closer to representing the system than to representing the people. It may be true that the citizens are not sufficiently qualified to be given greater influence in political decisions, through referenda for example, but the chief reason for this – and for the credibility gap between Parliament and people – is the lack of adequate information about political problems. Respect for politicians is not particularly pronounced; it is a fact, however, that government by the people presupposes respect for those elected by the people and *their* respect for the people as people – as distinct from mere voters.

CENTRALIZATION AND DECENTRALIZATION, BUREAUCRACY OR (LOCAL) DEMOCRACY

In principle local government elections are no different from national elections, since there, too, it is the parties who nominate the candidates. However the party lists are often supplemented by non-party lists of various kinds. It is characteristic that the poll for local elections is appreciably lower than for parliamentary elections and that more personal votes are cast. Linked with this is the fact that work in the local council is less party-political in nature than work in parliament.

The electorate usually plays a more active part in putting up its own programmes and candidates at local elections – but it is more passive when it comes to casting the vote. This is evidence of the dual tendencies for interest in local problems to be both greater and smaller than interest in national political problems. The lack of interest may be due to an impression that it is the central decisions that matter, also in relation to the local community. The initial interest may be evidence of a feeling that things should not be like this. At present, there is an obvious clash between the trend towards centralization demanded by national problems and the trend towards decentralization demanded by democracy, a move which appears necessary if people are to feel that they share responsibility for problem-solving, as they may well have to do if solutions are to be found.

Both these trends are evident in the reforms in local government passed in many countries over the last decade. In Denmark, in 1958, there were 1387 local districts in the country as against

275 now. The elimination of small districts has increased the distance between people and local authorities which were once a natural part of the local community. On the other hand larger administrative districts have a better chance of increased municipal independence from the state. The trend towards greater local autonomy is also visible in the fact that state support to local districts in Denmark has changed from operational grants for various local projects to block grants which the local council can spend as it wishes. If this opportunity to take independent measures is to lead anywhere the local districts will have to be even larger than they are now. Besides there is a conflict between the desire for (local) autonomy and the need for equality: real freedom for the local council must inevitably result in variations from district to district.

Until now the trend towards centralization has been by far the stronger; it is reinforced by technical and economic developments which favour the large at the expense of the small in every field of life: large-scale farming, chain stores, business takeovers, the closure of small institutions, population growth in the towns and depopulation of the rural areas, especially the small islands. 'It may be assumed that habitation of many of the smallest islands is being abandoned, and as a result of a number of interesting quasi-reservations will come into being' (note from an official body in the Danish Ministry of the Environment, dated 1973).

This trend has an adverse effect on (local) democracy in that it increases the distance between the people and the economic and political power base. The realization that the trend is also ecologically damaging and that 'small is beautiful' has become more general since the onset of the economic recession. In the last few years a counteractive tendency has grown stronger: citizens' meetings, local residents' associations and environmental movements are evidence of this. Politically it should lead to stronger local autonomy and closer ties between the electors and the elected so that the people really feel that they are being represented by the political bodies which a majority now sees as organs of 'state' and 'municipality'.

It is of course possible to reform the parliamentary *modus operandi*, to improve the working conditions of the members, to make parliament a forum for real decisions and not just for vote-casting, to bring together proposed laws and analyze their likely effects on society as a whole before they are adopted (computer technology and better expert assistance should make this possible), to improve communications between parliament and people, to make more use of referenda and public hearings, and so on. All these measures, however, are not enough to break the dominance of political parties and organizations; that would take a change in the electoral system so that the vote for a party was partly replaced by a vote for a local person. Effective local government also demands the existence of local districts so large that the population provides adequate support for institutions like hospitals, educational and research centres, etc. The best way to ensure proper cooperation between district and state is to provide representation for the district in parliament. Interest in politics would be stimulated if local and parliamentary elections were combined so that party representatives elected by the proportional representation system (as they are in Denmark) were complemented by local representatives elected by the majority vote system. Local councillors should form a majority in parliament.

The term 'local democracy' is a recent arrival in Denmark, a slogan which in itself expresses a protest against the tendency for democracy in a centralized and bureaucratic social system to recede into the distance. But the phrase does not denote anything other than democracy; indeed, the concept has no direct antithesis and 'democratic centralism' (as referred to in the new constitution of the Soviet Union) is a contradiction in terms. Even in a democratic society a strong tendency to centralize emanates from the central administration. It is therefore a precondition for (local) democracy that the power of the (distant) bureaucracy be limited. The starting point should be a 'criterion of proximity': all social tasks should be carried out as closely as possible to the individual citizen. The burden of proof should lie with those who wish for more centralization.

THE MEANS OF GOVERNMENT

It is parliament which makes laws and the government which rules according to them, although the actual wording of legislation is usually carried out by civil servants in the ministries. The law is administered by the judiciary and the instruments of the judiciary, the police force and the courts ensure that it is observed.

It goes without saying that the less a society needs to use the police and courts the better it is functioning. The term 'police state' is applied to a society in which there is total control and in which very little is left to be determined by the individual citizen. Countries where there is no parliament consisting of freely elected representatives and where the press is controlled by the government are effectively police states. The police state is generally characterized by a large bureaucracy and by minutely detailed legislation – if not still marked by a primitive form of despotism.

On the one hand law and justice protect the citizen from those in power. The constitutional state has evolved historically out of an endeavour to curb despotism. On the other hand law and justice are still part of the machinery of power and control that protects the social order against the citizen's taking the law into his own hands; and the laws which are intended to prevent antisocial acts may end up preventing social ones. In this, as in other areas, quantity (of laws and regulations) may have an adverse effect on quality (of legislation).

Respect for law and justice is more essential than law and justice themselves. The greater the respect the fewer laws are needed. In a close community other people's disapproval of undesirable behaviour is often punishment enough; people will control themselves and others according to unwritten laws. In a sense there is a contradiction between two facets of democracy, the first being that democracy actually means government by the people and the second that the existence of democracy involves a judicial system which is an instrument of government over people. And this contradiction emerges as a conflict between two trends. It is a major democratic principle that there must be equality before the law, but a judicial system which treats everybody alike (i.e. disregards individual, local, social and economic differences) can easily come to be seen as an impersonal, even inhuman, machine. By not taking variations into account it will *not* treat everyone alike but deal harder with the weakest in society.

The European liberal democracy resulted from a revolt against the kind of state that discriminated between people according to their rank. However, the revolt was directed not solely against the feudal state but generally against the right of the state to meddle in the lives of its citizens. Curiously enough, liberalists and marxists are in principle agreed that the power of the state should be as restricted as possible and that the autonomy of the citizen should be as comprehensive as possible. Marxists see the state as an instrument of class control which must give way to the classless society over a transitional phase when the state becomes a tool for the hitherto oppressed majority ('the dictatorship of the proletariat'). However, there is no evidence that the state is 'fading away' in the communist countries; on the contrary the bureaucracy has grown more powerful: where people do not have the opportunity to govern themselves the machinery of government must be that much larger. The bureaucracy has also expanded in the Western societies where it is left to the state to neutralize conflicts between economic interest groups. It is part of the burdensome inheritance of liberalism that economic freedom has been regarded as a precondition for democratic freedom, and that democratic equality has not been realized in the form of economic equality but in the form of equality before the law, a concept which betrays a trend towards bureaucratic standardization.

There is thus a close link between economic inequality and bureaucracy, although the reactionary forces of old liberalism would regard the machinery of state as merely a barrier to economic freedom and not a consequence of it. At the same time it is true that centralist standardization is just as great a barrier to democratic self-government as economic inequality. It is therefore no coincidence that the 'state bureaucracy' has recently become as popular a target for attack as 'capital'.

These attacks have been partly based on social economic considerations, and partly directed against the trend towards a form of state tutelage which makes life difficult for people, particularly for the small shopkeeper. Some of the laws that serve the best causes, such as those relating to food and the environment, are so pedantically detailed in their regulations that they become a positive hindrance to normal human enterprise. (The Danish grocer, for example, is forbidden to sell milk unless the ceiling is of the required height and may not store beer crates directly on the floor because all foodstuffs must be raised above the ground, etc.) Similar criticism may be directed at the slow workings of the administrative machine, the large number of channels through which a complaint or an application must pass. An application to change a school holiday has to go through the parent-teacher association, the education committee, local and regional authorities and back again through the same channels. Often permission will not reach base until long after the holiday has actually been changed. Finally, criticism can be levelled at the attitude of the public officials towards the citizen. The prevailing feeling is that disputes over the interpretation of laws and regulations are always settled to the disadvantage of the citizen, that civil servants are more eager to point out to people the duties they have failed to discharge than the rights they have failed to claim or possibly not known about. Computerization has increased the tendency to regard the administration as an impersonal machine; so, too, has the traditional form of official correspondence which is always full of stiff and authoritarian formulations but seldom answers questions or states reasons for decisions in ordinary, comprehensible language. The civil service, which all things considered ought to be just that, a service for the citizen, is seen as an instrument of control. It is typical of the whole problem that the ordinary citizen has to seek professional help from accountants, solicitors, social workers, etc., in his or her struggles with the authorities. It may also be typical that savings in the public sector are reflected in staff reductions in the actual service functions, in the postal services, the railways and in pre-school education.

The greatest sources of annoyance, of course, are the rising rates of taxation and excise duty and the zealous tax authorities. The number of disputes over taxation increases along with the rise in tax rates and it may take several years for a case to be decided. In this connection there is much evidence to suggest that respect for law and justice is very limited; many people feel greater respect for those who can play the tax authorities at their own game or evade taxation altogether, and they will be less indignant over a tax evader who is in fact appropriating part of public funds than over a poor thief who offends against private property. Indeed the thief will usually be punished comparatively harder than the tax evader. This point leads on to the sanctions which society employs against offenders. We can take the 'poor thief' as an example of the difference in treatment actually produced by the principle of equality under the law. A single mother of three children who worked as a night cleaner in a china factory in Copenhagen was tempted to steal a china figurine for a 'fence'. This was the first in a series of similar thefts lasting over a period of two to three years. She was sentenced to two and a half years in prison. The prosecution appealed against the sentence and got it increased to three years. She was retained in custody for nine months without permission to see her children. Her previous history was given as follows: 'Second eldest of six brothers and sisters in a working class family. Started working in a factory at 14. Pregnant at 17 and again at 19. Wretched housing conditions. Night work as cloakroom attendent and cleaner.'

A woman who is prompted by hardship to steal things which nobody suffers directly by losing is punished not only for her act of theft but, in reality, for her hardship. Society steps in, not to assist her in her need, but to deter further robberies; it protects the china factory against the woman. There is no consideration for the woman or her children. It is thought unjust that people should go unpunished simply because their circumstances are difficult. The best that can be done, in mitigation, is to shorten the sentence, a step not apparently considered by the court in this case. If hardship does not excuse theft then economic well-being cannot be regarded as a reason for making punishment more severe. In principle everybody is punished equally harshly for the same crime although the background to the crime may be widely different.

The fact that equality before the law fails to benefit the weakest is less remarkable when one considers that law and justice are there to protect the existing order which the strongest naturally have most to gain by maintaining. The judiciary is nearly always drawn from the upper classes and has no personal experience of the social conditions from which criminal behaviour usually arises. Generally speaking it is the well-to-do who pass judgement on the poor, the highly educated who pass judgement on the poorly educated. Legal experts do not figure among those who have worked hardest to remove the social causes of criminality. The medical experts who may be called in to assist the court and are instrumental in prisoners being given treatment rather than punishment where they consider that offenders have not been accountable for their actions, can subsequently seldom do anything other than adapt their patients to the same wretched conditions in which they were living before.

The best way to avoid recurrence of the crime, which is supposedly the purpose of punishment, is by improving the conditions of those concerned; the worst way is by segregating them into the company of other 'criminals'. Adjustment to life in the community becomes that much harder. Punishment only serves to confirm the representatives of the establishment in their belief that society is good enough as it is and that there is something wrong with anyone who does not thrive in it. In many cases, treatment in an institution, which is the only alternative to punishment, acquires the nature of an indefinite sentence and it is only warranted when those concerned are a positive danger to themselves or their surroundings.

The humane alternative is not to deprive people of responsibility for their actions but to pay proper regard to their background, which only those who know them can do. Breaches of the law should in principle be dealt with as a private dispute between the offender and the offended party; and if they are unable to reach a settlement then the vast, impersonal machinery of justice should not automatically come into operation and grind human destinies into the ground. If the ultimate ideal is that people should control themselves and one another through their attitudes, disapproval or approval, and if we accept as a fundamental principle that the offender should be able to return to the community, then judgement should be passed on the offence in that part of the community where it was committed and not by professionals but by ordinary people who feel jointly responsible for what happens in the future. Here, as in other areas of social life, the professional classes should be advising, not making decisions. The Norwegian criminologist Nils Christie has argued in his book *How close a society?* (*Hvor tett et samfunn?*) for a reform of the judicial process along these lines: 'If we seriously believe that people should be allowed to control themselves we must create decision models that can be used by ordinary people.' The current argument *against* lay judges and *for* professional judges is that people in general are more vindictive than objective experts. However this is only true when the people know nothing of the background to the case and when feelings are whipped up (usually by the mass media). 'Hatred and demands for severe penalities seem largely to arise when there is a lack of information and when there is no sense of proximity to the crime and the criminal.' A greater local share in responsibility for those who go astray gives the deviant a much better chance of returning to the community and is also the best form of prevention. Decentralization of the judiciary is essential for the democratization of society.

Decentralization of the machinery of administration is equally important. Where there is conflict between the desire for equality (under the law) and the need for self-determination, that equality which is not in fact justice but standardization must give way. If democratic equality is to be realized it must be in the economic rather than the legal sphere.

One reason why the administrative jungle has grown is the fact that legal provisions and regulations relating to different areas of life are not coordinated and frequently counteract one another. A second reason is that attempts to solve small problems are often made at the highest level and not at a local level where such problems can still be overcome. National planning must be confined to dealing with national political problems. Planning that can be carried out on a level closer to the citizen must not be dealt with by a central administration. However, when analyzing the causes of the growth in bureaucracy one should distinguish between factors such as poor coordination which can be removed from within the existing system and factors arising from the conflicts of interest inherent in the social system; these last can only be removed by a radical modification of that system.

The vast centralist machine is evidence of a lack of confidence in people's ability to exercise self-control. The abundance of penalties in legislation, of rules governing appeal procedure and of complaints courts would seem to be based on a picture of social life as a kind of battlefield in which the citizens are suspect individuals lacking the sense of responsibility which must underlie government by the people. Respect for law and justice is not increased by the number of legal provisions; mistrust is reciprocated by mistrust. But mistrust, self-interest and envy do not create a good socio-psychological basis for improvement. When there is a greater tendency to take the law into one's own hands, the demand for 'law and order' also becomes greater. Not everyone who takes action against the established order is fighting to improve society, not everyone who takes justice into his own hands is fighting for justice, but they may be provoking a reaction which is the first step towards a police state. Mistrust of the authorities can be justified up to a point, but not when every form of authority is challenged; criticism of the machinery of government can be justified up to a point, but not when it undermines every form of control, including the ability to control oneself.

Decentralizing the political and administrative system will impose greater demands on the citizen, but also on the politician whose opportunities for personal contact with constituents are at present few and who does not always possess the necessary insight into social relations. More direct contact between politicians and those they represent may be expected to encourage both sides to do their best.

THE EDUCATION SYSTEM

An extended democracy, of which the aims and assumptions are that the individual plays a more active part, requires a change in attitude. But a change in attitude presupposes a process of social change which in its turn influences the people. Obviously reforms in the educational system are particularly important when it comes to preparing future generations for social change. But it is here that the dilemma facing the education system lies, for the traditional purpose of education and training is to introduce the young to the values of existing society and qualify them to serve in that society. Education and training are thus conservative social functions, and the education system is also conservative in its structure. Each section of the system has evolved more or less independently of the rest; and once some particular educational field has defined itself there are interest groups which will rally round it and fight to strengthen its position. What internal relations there are have been established chiefly by higher education imposing a series of demands on the more elementary areas. This discourages innovation from below and is the reason why it has been so difficult to introduce a form of primary schooling where there is a greater emphasis on practical subjects.

Underlying these problems are the facts, first that disagreement about the aims and development of society is reflected in disagreement about the purposes of education, and second that doubts about traditional values and diminished respect for social authorities lead in their turn to a crisis of authority in the schools – and even more conspicuously in the universities. The involvement of all associated groups in the management of higher education establishments regardless of their professional competence and experiments with new kinds of basic education less rigorously divided into subjects and with less emphasis on the individual are just two examples of ways in which the education system can be made more democratic. To a certain extent, however, this type of democratization has turned wherever it has been tried into politicization and this has led to counter-demands for tighter laws governing university administration, stricter examination requirements and so on. Efforts to democratize should not be halted, however, just because they can be abused by power groups during the period of transition. If the greatest possible self-determination is a goal of democracy, it would be self-contradictory to deprive the educational institutions of their autonomy. On the other hand, dominance by organizations has as little to do with representative democracy in the institutions as it does in society at large.

Nor should lapses in development overshadow the fact that the youth and student revolutionary movements helped to start a trend towards better liaison between students and teachers, between different faculties and between school and society. All in all, however, this has had more influence on the educational debate than on the educational system.

The general move towards centralization has left its mark on education in the closing down of small schools, the desire to totally abolish the apprenticeship system, stricter admission and examination regulations, and so on. At the same time 'greater autonomy' and 'increased interest in the local community' are becoming popular slogans. Pupils are bussed from their local community to central schools though they ought to be receiving part of their schooling in that local community. Theoretical teaching would be more acceptable if pupils could come into contact with more aspects of community life and learn by their own experience during school hours. This would make school more rewarding for most children, and in particular for those who have difficulty in keeping up with the demands of formal teaching. There is evidence that this has been recognized, for instance, in those sections of the Danish Primary Education Act relating to job experience and practical training, although these rules conflict to a certain extent with labour legislation prohibiting children under 15 from having commercial jobs. As in many other areas, a reaction against the abuse of child labour has led not only to a suppression of the most unfortunate aspects but to a suspension of the entire case.

The preamble to the 1975 Danish Primary Education Act speaks of 'the all-round development of the individual pupil'. This implies that there should be an emphasis not solely on academic knowledge and intellectual ability but equally on children's emotional and physical development, their ability to work together and their practical skills. In fact practical subjects have been run down, music teaching leads a shadowy existence and physical training is generally limited to two gymnastic classes a week. We have not managed to break away from the traditional emphasis on theoretical learning although many children and young people have other talents which cannot be developed within the present framework. There are complaints about poor standards in writing and arithmetic; there are no complaints about the lack of practical skills. It is bad teaching practice always to be attacking people's weaknesses instead of giving them a chance to develop their strengths, so why are no conclusions drawn from this experience? Allowing children to demonstrate what they can do increases their self-respect and this, in turn, has a crucial influence on the benefits of their whole schooling.

There should be greater emphasis in all parts of the education system on a combination of theoretical education and practical work. Youth unemployment could, and should, be the basis for efforts in this direction. In 1977, there were 50-60,000 young people in Denmark between the ages of 15 and 24 out of work. Many of them went straight from school onto unemployment pay, and the problem is no less acute for being an international one. A member of the U.S. presidential education committee has stated that 'the U.S.A. is the first country in history able to increase production with no need to use the 15-17 year olds.' More and more young people in the coming years will be asking what their schooling and training is for when society does not need them anyway.

Various Danish experiments carried out during the 1970s have shown that young people who feel uncomfortable in the traditional school system are capable of surprising achievements when it comes to real work. It is this fact which ought to be governing the choice of school system. Where there are no opportunities to participate in the production sector in the local community, possibilities ought to exist for the creation of work centres in which practical production problems and teaching are synthesized. Projects in the centre could be chosen to match and form part of local undertakings, stimulating and serving educational, social and cultural innovation.

It must be recognized that the education system still functions to a large extent as a filter, enabling the fittest children to survive the highest exams to qualify themselves for the highest and most highly paid jobs in society. Part of the selection process has already taken place before the pupils themselves 'choose' which training and jobs they wish to undertake. For by allowing a comparatively small number selected from the more disadvantaged classes access to the top rung of the educational pyramid on an equal footing with its own children the elite is actually augmenting itself in what appears to be an equitable way. Social bias in the admission of students to higher education was the justification for raising the school-leaving age; but extended schooling for everybody is not the right way to iron out social differences. The proper means is to level out wage differentials so that choices of training and employment are not determined by economic privilege and self-interest but by other interests.

Real equality of educational opportunity does not mean that everybody should receive the same (higher) education and compete for the same (high) positions, but that there should be a 'multiplicity of environments, methods of upbringing and educational trends to suit the different abilities of different people' (Th. Dobzhansky). And this can be achieved by decentralizing education to the local communities and by combining theoretical education and practical training. What this means is that colleges of higher education should not grow into small cities of their own but should be split up into local research and training centres which could then influence development in the various regions, for example by offering adult education. Competition for qualifications through the education system has reinforced the trend towards lengthy training, which frequently proves to be of questionable value in a society undergoing constant change. In some fields extended education leads to overqualified people taking jobs from those who have been trained to do them. In a democratic society it is important that everyone, including the students with special talents, should be given the best possible educational conditions, but the kind of specialization necessary for the few who reach the top of the tree must not work down through the whole system and turn schooling into an ordeal for the many.

For years there has been controversy about how much of people's behaviour is determined by heredity and how much by environment. Human behaviour varies from one culture to another, but this does not preclude the existence of a common pattern of human need which may be more or less fulfilled in different societies. We know that there is a defined period in a child's life when he or she is particularly susceptible to the acquisition of language, and it is probably true in many other areas as well that the full development of faculties (such as the ability to cooperate and identify) is contingent on stimulation at the right time. The aim of education and training must be to provide this stimulus and not to condition children for specific functions in society. Forecasts about the future requirements of society are unreliable in our unsettled times and the idea that school pupils can acquire skills for life is an outdated one. The transition from a school which places emphasis on 'all-round development' to a society which does not may give rise to difficulties, and these difficulties reflect a real discrepancy between the democratic ideals people are brought up to believe and cherish and the norms current in society.

We have seen that the problems of modern society are growing, that the machinery of government is expanding without producing more effective solutions to the problems or more effective government. And this is due to the fact that there are conflicts of interest inherent in the politico-economic system which cannot be resolved within that system. But the basic conflict appears to be between the needs of the social system itself and the needs of people. In the last decade the ecology shock has shown us that people cannot exploit the physical resources of nature for any purpose they choose without paying the penalty. We must also recognize that people cannot be exploited and conditioned for any purpose at all without injury to both body and soul.

CHAPTER THREE

THE FOUNDATION

PEOPLE ARE NOT MERELY PRODUCTS OF SOCIETY

The goal of marxism-leninism is 'the complete satisfaction of the material and spiritual needs of all members of society'. There can hardly be a better goal for a humane society, as most people would surely agree. On the other hand most people would disagree about what those material and spiritual needs are, and as the Foundation of Marxism-Leninism puts it, 'It is senseless to conjecture about what shape these needs will take in concrete form . . . Human needs are not something rigid and unchangeable, they are constantly growing and developing . . . This is the reason why the communist order sets itself the task of satisfying the ever-increasing needs of all members of society.'

To state that it is senseless to surmise about the needs of 'communist people' is just a euphemistic way of saying that people's needs are created by social development; there is no suggestion that society ought to develop in such a way as to satisfy those needs people already have, which are perfectly open to conjecture. Although it ought to be self-evident that society should be so organized as to meet people's needs, the position in practice – and in marxist-leninist theory – is quite the opposite. People are regarded as products of social evolution; marxist-leninist psychology is still coloured by the doctrines of the physiologist I. P. Pavlov concerning the influence of environment on human and animal behaviour: 'Everything can be changed for the better as long as the correct conditions are realized.'

The dominant school of psychology in the U.S.A., the behaviourist school, also maintains that environmental influences are of much more significance for people's behaviour than their innate dispositions and needs. The practical conclusion of this theory is that people can be 'reinforced' through purposive influence (operant conditioning) in the kind of behaviour which is considered socially expedient. The reasons for people's behaviour lie not in their own will but in the environment. In a sense there is no difference between human beings and external, inorganic nature. 'Physics did not advance by looking more closely at the jubilance of a falling body or biology by looking at the nature of vital spirits, and we do not need to try to discover what personalities, states of mind, feelings, traits of character, plans, purposes, intentions, or the other perquisites of autonomous man really are in order to get on with a scientific analysis of behaviour.' So writes the behavioural psychologist B. F. Skinner in his book *Beyond Freedom and Dignity* and he maintains that self-determination and freedom are luxuries which modern society cannot afford.

With the theory that human beings are only what they are made into, the way lies open for technological control of people, a process for which computer technology can supply effective means. This will of course lead to a gulf between the people who are *made into* whatever is required by the machinery of control and those who represent the machinery, although the latter will also in fact be *made into* a part of the machinery and its impersonal, even inhuman, reasoning. Decision makers in the most advanced nations have already surrendered part of their competence to computers, although they preserve the illusion that they are still responsible for formulating the questions put to the machines and evaluating the answers. It was computers which decided targets and quantities of bombs to be dropped on Vietnam: all Secretary of State Kissinger could do was to deplore the horrors suffered by so many people. The vast data system in the Pentagon has more authority than any government official, because it cannot be accused of harbouring prejudices and people who are totally dependent on its machinery can be presumed to be moulded in its image. As one scientist has expressed it, 'It is possible to see human beings themselves as the products of an evolutionary process directed towards the production of robots.'

The computer itself is well-suited to confirm people's belief in the inevitable requirements of development and to quieten the

78

voice of conscience, i.e. to eradicate humanity. With the use of computer technology it is possible to exercise total control over labour in the work place and over people in society as a whole; the enormous problems of society demand an effective technology for control, even though the very feasibility of such technology is an obstacle to any solution of problems which might make control unnecessary.

The theory that people are only products of their environment and can therefore be made to conform to anything at all is attractive not only to those in power but also to the social revolutionaries, simply because of its social implications. One of the great humane advances has been the recognition of the social causes of criminality; a similar recognition of the extent to which illness is socially determined can hardly be said to have made the same headway as yet. To draw conclusions from this recognition must mean to improve the environment so that the causes of disease are prevented.

If we then go on to ask how this should be done, there is only one answer: by establishing a society where people's needs are satisfied to the extent that illness is avoided. And the next question follows naturally from the first: which needs and how can they best be satisfied? – a question which the marxist-leninists and behaviourist theory of environment refuses to ask. And this refusal also averts the question of what a society, i.e. its authorities, may be permitted to do with and to people.

If *everything* is determined by society there is no self-determin-ation. If people do not have the right to be their natural selves, the only right they have is given them by society. If it is not people themselves but only environment which is responsible for their thoughts and actions, then society might presume, for example, to remove them from their present environment and place them in another where they will receive the 'correct' treatment for their deviant ideas.

A BIASED CONCEPTION OF MANKIND

If the view that everything is determined by society can actually be considered 'progressive' it is partly because it is considered conservative to view people as so incorrigible by nature that no appreciable improvement in human society is ever possible. Considering how much emphasis conservative people have in fact laid on authoritarian education, it would seem that conservative thinking is peculiar, less for its belief in human incorrigibility, than for its faith in human corrigibility: nature is not good enough but must be cultivated. It was this attitude which once gave rise to primitive people being labelled uncivilized. Christian tradition holds that people are naturally sinful, and when Darwin first published his biological theory of evolution, the stress he laid on human kinship to other animals, and in particular to apes, caused enormous outrage. Nowadays it is often considered reactionary to emphasize this kinship, partly because the Darwinian theory of natural selection has been used as an argument to prove that economic competition is also natural.

The study of humans has been dominated by ideological viewpoints because there is no one science dealing with human nature which produces results as cogent as those of the natural sciences. We cannot conduct observations of a human being who has not been influenced by some form of society, which means that the experimental sciences will tend to disregard anything that is common to all human beings and to treat their innate nature as an abstraction. However, it is so obvious that human beings are products both of nature and of their society, both biological and social creatures, that there must be specific reasons or motives for disregarding their biological or social aspects. The very basis for this sterile ideological dispute would appear to be an innate tendency to think in opposites.

It takes a great deal of independent and mature thinking to override the primitive tendency to divide the world into right and wrong, good and evil, friends and foes, as we are induced to do by the whole of Western dualism. Indeed, it was rebellion against this rigid logic that led the philosopher Hegel to create his 'dialectical' logic which emphasizes that opposites are relative (not absolute) and different aspects of the same thing. Marx, Engels and Lenin subscribed to this way of thinking and it is sad that their successors should have become some of the most extreme proponents of obstinate and dogmatic either-or ideas, or *idées fixes*.

If this primitive either-or logic (which is more pronounced in European than in Oriental thought) really is innate in us, it merely goes to show that not all innate tendencies are appropriate in the modern world. And it is, of course, for this precise reason that the 'progressive' minds who want to organize society along humane lines, prefer to overlook any innate tendencies which do not fit into their view of the social order. The fact that a society elaborated on the basis of such a partial theory will never be humane is another matter: if no attention is paid to the more difficult aspects of the theory, they will make the theory more difficult to put into practice.

HUMANS ARE BIOLOGICAL CREATURES AS WELL

It is a manifestation of primitive either-or logic to think that the human being is either an animal like other animals or not an animal at all, or in other words that human behaviour is either innate or a product of society. The human infant is born in such an undeveloped state that it remains dependent on its parents for much longer than the young of any other species. While animal behaviour is for the most part 'programmed' by genes, the human infant is brought up during its long period of dependence to conform to the behaviour patterns prevailing in its cultural environment. However, to deduce from this that innate characteristics are so insignificant as to be negligible is to overlook the fact that the human infant's extended period of dependence on its parents and its great ability to learn are themselves biologically determined, determined by the development of the brain which accompanied the evolution of the human species.

The human parents' urge to care for the child for much longer than animal parents – the parental instinct – is also biologically programmed. Unlike animals, whose touchingly solicitous care for their young is followed by total lack of interest once the young can look after themselves, people may find it hard to let their children go; and this is partly because of their strong, innate need to care and partly because of a family pattern which once gave parents a kind of proprietary right over their children and which has since undermined their authority. There are, in fact, biological, cultural *and* social causes for all the basic conflicts.

Even the elementary conflict between the modern social system and the innate needs of human beings, however, raises such enormous theoretical and practical problems that it is easier to disregard it. Once it has been recognized that human beings are biological creatures, it must also be recognized that, like all other creatures, they bear the marks of their biological inheritance. The traits which have been passed on are those which have survival value for the species, but these traits were acquired in circumstances totally different from those in which human beings live in modern society. The human species spent 99% of its existence in small, stone-age communities and modern men and women must therefore have been born with needs and dispositions which are scarcely recognized in mass society.

Ideological theories and political systems which do not pay heed to natural needs and rights are committing an offence against human nature and creating frustration and aggression, thereby increasing the need for government and control. A system of government in conflict with nature must become more and more totalitarian to be effective; it may even reach a point where it becomes necessary to manipulate troublesome inherited characteristics so as to make people toe the line. There is a tendency in technological development, moreover, to make human beings the subject of decisions, treatment and manipulation. Conservative ideologies based on the notion that people are naturally wicked and must therefore be disciplined and progressive ideologies based on the notion that people are not products of nature and can therefore be made to conform to anything at all are both equally good, or equally bad, at suppressing what is human.

MORALITY, THE ORIGINAL INSTRUMENT OF CONTROL

The variation in moral standards from culture to culture, society to society, and era to era, is frequently used to support the argument that human behaviour is determined far more by environment than by innate nature. The difference between human beings and animals, however, is not that people lack innate urges, needs and dispositions but that they have no one innate system of standards. People are not programmed by nature for a specific mode of existence but are by nature creators of civilization and thus predisposed to shape their own existence and to exercise self-control. Without the control of instinctive urges no society can be formed, and the original means of control is *morality*.

With the help of moral standards people control each other and themselves, and these standards will continue to exercise a direct influence provided that they do not appear to be arbitrarily chosen but seem deeply rooted in the fundamental nature of life, in the world order. For then it becomes sacrilege to infringe upon them. Anyone who does so is dishonoured; the effect of others' disapproval on the person who accepts the communal norms is much stronger than the effect of severe punishment on the person who does not. But it is only a 'close' community which can be governed by ethical norms; the greater the distance between the members of a society and the social authorities, the more legal provisions there will be and the greater the bureaucracy becomes. There is an upper limit to the 'natural' size of a community.

Social morality has a dual function: it serves not merely to restrain antisocial inclinations but also to keep up people's spirits and to give their life meaning. Life has meaning for those who feel in harmony with something outside themselves, with the nature of existence, with the community, or, at the least, with a group of people who share the same customs or tasks. In poor communities the vast majority of people had compelling reasons for leading a thrifty life; and the prevailing standards, which were officially based on religious rather than economic arguments, made thrift and abstinence into moral achievements. In the boom society there are no compelling reasons for renouncing anything, since the uneconomical economy of society demands increasing consumption; and it may simply look as if the meaning of existence is to acquire ever more new possessions. The old Christian-based morality has lost its influence, although the present moral 'liberation' is still very much in the nature of a reaction against the old standards and there have been no new standards to succeed them. The feeling of purposelessness and meaninglessness is more strongly marked.

ECONOMY AND MORALITY

Which moral standards will answer the needs of modern society? Social morality serves to maintain society in its existing shape, and it is not necessary to be a marxist to realize that 'only that which society can accommodate economically at any given point in time will be called moral', as the conservative Danish writer, Jacob Knudsen, put it in 1906. But when the economy of modern industrial society is bringing about a progressive annihilation of natural resources, statements along the lines that 'what is good for the social economy is also good for people' are bound to be oversimplifications. In a reasonably harmonious society there is no difference between what is good for the social order and what people see as good for themselves. When it comes to modern society, however, J. M. Keynes had no hesitation in declaring that 'foul is useful and fair is not'. The economy of modern society demands selfish attributes like greed, avarice and ruthlessness which were deadly sins in the old Christian morality. So imbued are we, however, with the idea that what is moral is also good (and we tend to speak only of one morality and not several moralities), that we find it impossible to rank the selfish attributes among the moral virtues.

Assuming, then, that people may have a conception of good and evil which is different from that which their society has taught them, where can their conception have come from? It is not out of the question that it has come from themselves, or in other words that something in people reacts against a social order which does not allow them to live by their moral aspirations. (Indignation is a very spontaneous reaction, it requires no previous study of comparative history or sociology.) The fundamental moral ideas were first formulated in the 6th century BC by five wise men who, as Arnold Toynbee says, 'are today still influencing mankind, either directly or indirectly, more than any human being who is now alive' (*Mankind and Mother Earth*, p.177); and the remarkable thing is that each of these men formulated his ideas in his own cultural group independently of the others. They were Zarathustra in Iran, Buddha in India, Confucius in China, Deutero-Isaiah in Israel and Pythagoras in Graeco-Italy. The notion central to their philosophy is that human beings can be above society: they do not need the mediation of society and its priests to communicate with inner spiritual reality. Something is good or evil in itself irrespective of the judgment of social morality; and according to this higher morality the five wise men passed judgment on their society. The focus for their condemnation was the tendency to set economic values above existing natural values.

In the beginning, for the primitive mentality, there was no difference between a good man and a rich man: riches were taken as evidence of divine favour (as in the Old Testament). In the urban civilization, with its trade and its monetary economy, however, wealth comes to be seen more as evidence of human enterprise and greed than as a sign of divine good grace. As the five wise men saw it, the economic expansion which leads to class divisions within society is a deviation from nature; and the primary notion of humanism, namely that human value is unaffected by social standing, that it is intrinsic, was formulated as a protest against economic development. From its earliest days, the traditional wisdom of mankind has turned its face against any form of development that prizes goods above the good, differentiates between people and makes the driving force a desire for wealth rather than care for one's fellow human beings.

The desire for wealth did not become a major driving force until a very recent point in history during the period of transition from a static agricultural to a more dynamic commercial society. In Europe this phase occurred during the 18th century at a time when modern democratic ideas were also being formulated in protest against discrimination, against the privileges of rank and against restrictions on freedom. But the spirit behind these new ideas was completely different, one might almost say opposite:

1. While the kind of development which is powered by economic interests was once regarded as a deviation from nature it now comes to be seen as the natural course of affairs.
2. While the five wise men directed their criticism primarily against the greed and insatiability of the rich, 'self-interest' now comes to be seen as the natural driving force of human beings and as socially valuable.
3. While great private fortunes were once seen as the cause of social injustice, now, in the era of revolution, private property comes to be regarded as a natural human right on a par with equality and freedom.

With the onset of the industrial revolution there is thus a total reappraisal of moral values: foul, as Keynes put it, becomes socially useful. But this does not mean that the old Christian morality has been superseded by the new morality of greed; on the contrary, in those societies which are both capitalist and Christian and where people are required to be both self-seeking and humble, the two moral doctrines prevail side by side. There is one morality for the business man and another for the private person, and many of the classic entrepreneurs from the pioneering days of capitalism lived up to this form of dual morality. As the sociologist Max Weber has shown in a celebrated book, there is a connection between 'the spirit of capitalism and the protestant ethic'. It is morally reprehensible to use one's own property as a support but not to acquire it in the first place nor to let it generate further wealth; wealth must not be the prime objective of work, but its result, its reward. So the 'ascetic' entrepreneur can still see a connection between goods and the good; a rich man has not only luck but also God on his side. Socially useful work is particularly pleasing in the sight of God; work ennobles those, too, whose labours do not produce great wealth, and if the material rewards are not high then at least labour has its intrinsic moral rewards.

With the gathering tide of class conflict there has been a tendency for business morality to apply to the upper classes, the morality of thrift to the lower classes who, as the good book puts it, have been laying up treasure for themselves in heaven by going without on earth. Rising affluence has led to the triumph of self-interest in all classes and professions, while the morality of thrift has begun to look more like bad conscience. Admittedly it has become harder to believe in Keynes' words that 'Avarice and usury and precaution must be our gods for a little longer still' and that they will then lead us out of the 'tunnel of economic necessity' so that we can afford to see the fair as useful and the foul as harmful. By obeying these 'gods' we have turned against us those other divinities which the five wise men identified with nature, that is with the proper laws of existence. Nature's reaction to our economy may reveal that they and not the liberal economists are right. Ecological problems demand that we create a civilization that is in balance with nature.

Although human beings as creators of civilization can shape their own existence and organize society according to different standards, they cannot do so totally arbitrarily without turning nature against them. When large urban civilizations develop symptoms of decline even at their height it simply goes to show that the gap between a complex social system and human need can grow too great. The road to collapse is precisely the route indicated by Keynes: to let fair be socially harmful and foul socially useful.

SEXUAL MORALITY

When material goods were scarce most people had pressing reasons for abstaining and morality turned abstinence into moral gain. While drudgery in the service of self and of society passed for moral achievement, it was also morally profitable to suppress one's desires, particularly where they were strongest, in the sexual sphere. Social morality traditionally means sexual morality, and when we talk of loose morals or immorality what we mean is lechery.

While it was possible to identify self interest with common interest, it was impossible to overlook a radical opposition between the needs of society and the desires of the individual. It was therefore necessary to control the desires of the individual through sexual morality.

Sigmund Freud, who around the turn of the century reacted against his contemporary society's tendency to underestimate the importance of sexuality, and who in turn overestimated it, assumed that there must be an insuperable antagonism between the 'pleasure principle' and the 'reality principle'. As he saw it civilization itself was based on the repression of sexual instincts. Willing hands make light work, or in other words work is powered by desire; but according to Freud desire is converted or 'sublimated' into social productivity: what is allowed to manifest itself as 'desire' is withheld from society. Freud made as little distinction between working from desire and working from need as he did between self-control and repression. He presupposed the existence of a constant sum of psychic energy which he identified with sexuality (later adding a complementary but primordial 'death instinct' or 'aggression instinct'). But the sexuality Freud knew was that which his contemporaries refused to acknowledge, repressed sexuality.

For Freud normal development consisted in the body becoming gradually de-eroticized so that pleasurable sensations came to be concentrated round the genital organs. But this kind of specificity is probably only normal in Western, Christian scientific culture which has sex on the brain and very little eros in the body. In the Christian tradition, which is strongest in Roman Catholic countries, sexual desire is 'not for pleasure alone' but serves society by ensuring its continuance. Since sexual relations without conception are not socially useful, the Catholic church regards them as being contrary to nature as well. What this actually means is that the non-sexual aspects of loving relationships, such as tenderness, consideration and sensitivity, are not seen as being particularly natural to human beings – which they of course are.

By perceiving all social relations as basically sexual, Freud totally overlooked the parental instinct which, unlike sexuality, is highly developed in human beings. Corresponding to the human baby's long period of dependence on its parents, and especially on its mother, there is an innate readiness to care for the child, an innate weakness for the weak so to speak, which has a far greater influence on human relationships than 'naked' sexuality.

When Freud wrote about 'civilization and its discontents' he characterized a civilization in which human beings have no opportunity to fulfil themselves according to their nature. However, there is a considerable gap between the recognition that no society can be established without the control of instinct and the assertion that there is an insuperable conflict between the needs of the individual and the demands of society so that civilization must necessarily acquire the nature of repression. Freud regarded sexual morality as rooted in the essence of life and not merely in the social economy; it never occurred to him to ask whether a rich society has to ask for the same sexual repression as a poor society.

Traditional sexual morality, although officially grounded in the commandments of God, was obviously based on economics – that underlying foundation has changed. Morality served chiefly to protect marriage and the family as institutions, and the family was originally a small-scale productive cooperative. The traditional occupations of housewife and maid servant, cooking, washing and cleaning have been considerably reduced over the last decades by an expanding service industry; one reason for this trend, and one of its results, is that more women are going outside the home to work. Women have become less economically dependent on men, and at the same time male parental authority has been appreciably diminished. This is partly a result of an economic and technical development that allows people to grow older in circumstances very different from those in which they were brought up. In modern society the raising of children is as much the business of the institution as of the home.

The family still has an economic function as a consumer unit, but as such it is not economical. 'When we are single we don't buy dish-washers, but as soon as there are two of us, we do,' writes the Danish author Suzanne Brøgger, and she gives many other examples of the importance of the nuclear family in the consumer society. The economist J. K. Galbraith writes that the family is no longer an economic necessity, 'with higher living standards it becomes, increasingly, a facilitating instrument for increased consumption' (*Economics and the Public Purpose*).

As long as increased consumption is in the interests of the social economy, however, the family will continue to have a social function, and to that extent so will the sexual morality that protects it. Yet there is no organic connection between increased consumption and marital fidelity; on the contrary, there is a connection between extra consumption in the one area and the other; new relationships, like new possessions, bolster self-respect. It is no longer felt that sexual morality is rooted in nature; it seems more natural to follow one's own desires (especially when there are now more efficient means of contraception than abstinence based on morality).

Marriage first entered a phase of crisis when people began to marry chiefly for emotional rather than social reasons. This led to greater expectations of marriage; when moral standards are undermined it becomes harder to find any meaning in life and people seek more ardently to find a meaning in their emotional relationships with the result that disappointment is often that much greater. It is these disappointed hopes of the 'one and only' which may tempt people to try their luck elsewhere. Sexual liberation is also characterized by a tendency to overvalue the sexual aspect of relations and undervalue the need for contact, a need which sexual morality demanded should be fulfilled within marriage. There is a greater strain on the pair relationship now that the family is losing its natural size of several generations and has shrunk to a mere 2-5 people who are still interdependent even though they seldom have much time for one another and rarely join forces to fulfil some important activity. Now that the social basis has changed the sexual morality which once protected the economically weakest, the women and children, has come, if anything, to protect proprietary rights over fellow human beings. The nuclear family, an instrument for increased consumption, can also be an obstacle to natural self-fulfilment.

A rich society must be able to make room for relationships which are not based on economic dependence. The Danish writer Jacob Knudsen who perceived, as we have mentioned above, that only that which society can accommodate economically will be called moral, thought that the state should take over the support of the child but not its upbringing. Marx and Engels, on the other hand, made a point of including the provision of state facilities for child rearing in their Communist Manifesto, in which they also predicted that the bourgeois family would disappear when private, capitalist ownership was abolished. Lenin wrote that 'a true liberation of women, real communism, begins in that place and at that time when the struggle of the masses begins . . . against the small-scale household,' – as if the small-scale household were the real enemy of communism. In the *Foundation of Marxism-Leninism*, the most important measures are named as 'the greatest possible development of forms of communal feeding, of various service institutions and all kinds of establishments for children.'

As everyone knows, the bourgeois family has not been abolished in the communist states, whether this is due to the fact that the family has a biological basis or to the fact that proprietorial relationships have not radically changed. The breakdown of the family has reached a more advanced stage in the capitalist countries where living standards are higher, norms less rigid and consciousness of rights more pronounced. The right of women to social and economic equality is one of the elementary requirements for democracy.

The psychological and social problems raised by the waning social importance of the family will not be solved by communal feeding or large institutions which only serve to make society and communal life more impersonal. We know that it is crucially important for a child to have physical contact with its mother during the first 24 hours of life and a close relationship with one person during the first two years if it is to be able to form close personal ties afterwards. The many-sided social needs of human beings are not satisfied in the enclosed nuclear family or in institutions where the only company may be people of the same age group or people with the same problems. The natural environment is still the extended family or family group comprising several generations. Above a certain size the family becomes an instrument for reduced consumption. Joint use of energy-consuming equipment and cooperation over energy-consuming tasks will become economic exigencies to such an extent that they may also become moral exigencies.

If sexual morality is to be perceived as rooted in life (and not just in the social economy) it must brand as immoral anything which hampers the capacity and desire of human beings for self-fulfilment. It is good not merely for the national economy but also for men and women that both sexes should be able to play a part in the whole of society and not just in their own allotted sphere of life. Those attributes which we designated above as being specifically human; consideration, tenderness and sensitivity, have traditionally been treated as specifically feminine. While woman has been socially repressed, man has been more restricted in his emotional development, not least by the classic concept of the 'real boy' who may be beaten but must not grizzle. The only psychological difference between the sexes on which researchers are reasonably agreed is that man is more aggressive than woman, and in a male-oriented, competitive society the desire to fight and possess is regarded as more a socially acceptable instinct than simple desire. There may be no economic basis in society for a different morality, but it will require a different morality to create a more humane and more economical society. In sexual relationships it is aggressivity and not desire that is bad; and attempts to prevent people from doing what they want when their actions harm nobody else are just as immoral as attempts to force people to do something they do not want. There is no good reason for forbidding or discriminating against any form of deviant sexuality – apart from the irrational fear that it may 'contaminate' a 'healthy' society. In this instance, too, the theory of environmental influence plays a reactionary role, both among Christian people who believe that young

91

persons can be seduced into homosexuality, and in some communist states where homosexuality is regarded as bourgeois decadence and punished accordingly.

THE WORK ETHIC

There is a traditional antithesis between pleasure and work. 'We were sent hither for work and not for pleasure and play', wrote the Danish poet Carsten Hauch. Sloth is one of Christianity's seven deadly sins – as is lust. This moral view forms a sharp contrast to the more psychological attitude expressed in the formula that willing hands make light work. In fact there are two completely different driving forces that motivate people to work: need and desire. But working from desire, which is easy as playing, is not recognized as real work. In Christian terms work also meant working to save the soul, and the more unpleasant the task the more purifying it was.

Needless to say, this kind of work ethic benefits those who do not themselves have to undertake the most unpleasant work but who have much to gain by getting the job done as cheaply as possible. In a society where there is no lack of labour but where most people lack sufficient physical exercise we should be able to afford a different attitude to work. Work may no longer be regarded as a *moral* achievement but it is still seen as a necessary evil, partly because jobs are expensive (for employers) and every attempt will therefore be made to reduce human labour, partly because the work is often dissatisfying for the workers (for the same reason). When people do not view work as a direct means of averting need, its meaning may be harder to appreciate unless the work is satisfying in itself.

Nevertheless the old work ethic is still so persuasive an influence that long periods of unemployment will frequently shake people's self-respect and the respect of others. The father of a family who stays home without any function is less impressive a figure than the person who returns home from some unknown place of work.

The unemployment problem has several different facets for those involved:

1. The economic problem, though this is less severe in the welfare state than it was in earlier times.

2. The social problem. The unemployed feel superfluous, society does not need them. This is not merely a question of social prejudice (the old work ethic), but also of a primordial desire to participate.

3. The psychological problem. It is satisfying to utilize one's abilities, frustrating not to be able to use them at all. There is evidence to suggest that recreational activities are only satisfying when they are recreational, and that once people have all the time in the world to devote to them they lose some of their attraction. 'The abolition of work' which has generally been seen as a utopian goal will not lead to greater human self-fulfilment as long as paid work alone is held in respect as being productive and socially useful.

Meanwhile there is an unmistakable trend in modern society towards reducing the time spent on actual production. The economist E. F. Schumacher has calculated that production accounts for about 3½% of total social time. Although both the right- and the left-wing place a higher value on the kind of productive work that creates assets for society (and as marxist theory would put it, 'surplus value') than they do on work in the public sector or service industries, Schumacher felt able to assert that 'the prestige carried by people in modern industrial society varies in inverse proportion to their closeness to actual production' (*Small is Beautiful*, p.125). As marxists see it, the explanation for this apparent contradiction is quite simply that productive labour *does* create surplus value and must therefore be paid as little as possible so that profits can be larger.

The discrepancy between the need of society, or more accurately of the private capitalist system, to reduce human labour, and the need of people to make themselves useful is particularly evident in the industrialization of agriculture. Agriculture is a highly important industry in many Western countries, and yet it employs only a very small percentage of the population. Mechanization, with its associated tendency to turn animals into machine components, has made agriculture more vulnerable to failure in energy supplies. The more reductions are made in manpower, of which there is a surplus, the greater the waste of resources, of which there is a shortage.

Now that we have reached a stage where socially useful work is not economically worth while for society, a radical change would appear to be necessary. Reducing the wage for the job is an obvious possibility, though only realizable if the job contains its own rewards, at least in part, and is not just a job with pay but a way of making oneself useful. It is this kind of amendment in the nature and status of work that can, and must, be made at a point in development where technical facilities *could* make human labour more human instead of rationalizing it away – and at the same time making production more irrational – as happens now.

EQUALITY AND DIFFERENCE

The extent to which the human image at any given point in time is dependent on that time is indicated by the fact that Freud in the Victorian era regarded sexuality as the innermost human driving force, whereas now, in a technically much more advanced society, the behavioural psychologists exclude feelings, intentions and so on completely from the 'scientific' analyses of behaviour. Since by doing so they accord no importance to innate instincts they must look for external motives for people's actions. People must be 'reinforced' in desirable behaviour so that the expectation of reward for their actions becomes their main incentive. Although it is possible to conceive of other forms of reward than wages, the wages system thus becomes central to the behaviourist society, in which people who have theoretically been created the same (according to the behaviourists) must be brought up very differently so that all the social functions will be fulfilled. People do not decide for themselves what they are going to do with their lives, since their behaviour is only the result of environmental influences; the decision, in other words, is made by those who have the power to influence them. Clearly however, conditioning of this kind must follow totally arbitrary criteria, for how can one argue that one human being should become an engineer and another a dustman when innate differences are neither stated nor accepted?

The survival of the human species and the ability to construct a society must, of course, have benefitted from the fact that talents are *not* distributed in equal measure to all. It is possible to imagine a division of labour which does not depend on external coercion but on inner compulsion and, for that matter, on practical considerations. Indeed a division of labour along these lines was practised in early forms of society. In modern industrial societies we are faced with a paradox. Division of labour is taken to absurd lengths; and specialization, which originates in pressure from economic interest groups and a one-sided educational system, does not primarily reflect opportunities for individuals to follow their own interests. Yet, at the same time, democratic dogma tells us that all people are born equal.

If all human beings really are born equal, in the sense that all differences are created by the environment, then it must surely be rather unjust to train people for different things. The demand for equality will only be fulfilled if all people are trained for precisely the same position in society; and true democracy will then be as Adolf Hitler described it when he promised that 'every German boy will march at the head of the nation', with the added proviso, of course, that this should apply to every German girl as well. On such an arbitrary, theoretical basis, the only course is in fact to reinforce individual people in different forms of behaviour through operant conditioning, to *create* inequality from the premise that all human beings are born equal.

If, on the other hand, people are actually born different, as independent individuals and not merely as undifferentiated raw material, there is less need for society to *make* differences. Social justice must then consist in equal opportunities for everybody to develop his or her different abilities, a course which would also benefit society since there would be a better chance of necessary social tasks being undertaken without external co-ercion or rewards. However, as soon as different values are accorded to different kinds of ability, society begins to discrimin-ate and to offend against the democratic concept of equality.

If, as all the evidence suggests, the existence of innate abilities implies a desire to use them, people will not need to be reinforced in socially desirable behaviour; it will usually be sufficient to remove the obstacles which hinder the free play of abilities, and these obstacles lie in social background, bad housing, discrimin-atory upbringing, over-specialized education, pressure from economic interest groups, bureaucratic administration, or, to put it briefly, in the lack of regard for individual needs.

If people do not have the opportunity to pursue their desires or interests, then obviously there will be no willing hands to lighten the work, and any tasks which cannot contain their own rewards will have to be remunerated or paid. Many strikes in recent years have been motivated by resentment that others receive higher wages for the same kind of work. In many cases the motive is not primarily economic, however, but psychological: it is injured pride. This is inevitable in a society that pays homage to democratic equality and yet evaluates people economically – placing the highest value on those people who have the most satisfying work. 'Were we not totally accustomed to such an arrangement,' writes J. K. Galbraith, 'it would seem remarkably bizarre.' The arrangement goes back to the days when it was the individual family which usually bore the economic sacrifice of training the children. Now that the state pays for higher education in many countries, there is no reason to reward the highest trained. The fact that we have not only different wages for the same work, but different wages for different work, is evidence of discriminatory treatment that is not democratic.

FORMS OF AGGRESSION

The controversy over how far the innate and the learned affect behaviour has been very fierce when it comes to discussing the fighting instinct (aggression) and the spirit of emulation (competition). Konrad Lorenz opened the debate when he stated in *On Aggression* that aggression, although regarded as 'bad', was originally good for some things, and still is when it takes the form of 'drive'. There must be a fighting spirit to attack a problem. But with the competitive society, which in Keynes' words has made 'foul useful', antisocial instincts have become overdeveloped and distorted. So Lorenz did not simply come down on the side of aggression; on the contrary, he came down against social relationships that encourage it. But just as Freud was accused by Wilhelm Reich of playing into the hands of a conservative ideology when he postulated the existence of a death instinct alongside the sexual life instinct, so, too, has Lorenz been blamed for playing the reactionary's game. His socially minded opponents have found it difficult to differentiate between the objective recognition of an instinct and the ethical acknowledgement of it. An innate predisposition is not socially justified by the fact that it is innate. What may have been expedient at some earlier point in the evolutionary history of the human species is not necessarily expedient in modern society.

We know that the human species evolved in a struggle with other species, that human societies have fought wars against one another and that 'the history of all hitherto existing society is the history of class struggles' *(Manifesto of the Communist Party)*. It is therefore improvident wishful thinking to deny human beings innate aggressive tendencies (which are not the same thing as innate aggression). Like animals, human beings are alerted by both fighting and fear instincts designed to protect them in circumstances of combat. They can, of course, deliberately control their impulses to fear and anger, particularly if their social norms prompt them to do so, but they do not deliberately become angry or afraid in the first place.

Just like other animal species, the human species has found it necessary to spread over wide areas so that not everybody is dependent on the same resources (as they are in modern society). Fighting over territory safeguards this dispersal. The desire to safeguard one's territory appears to be a primitive urge in humans and is readily observable in children.

Clearly, however, aggression and territoriality are only expedient up to a certain point. It benefits neither the species nor humanity if one nation oppresses another or if people murder one another. We know that animals (and this applies to wild animals more than to domestic cats, for example), have an instinctive inhibition about mutilating or killing members of their own species with whom they unconsciously share mutual interests, just as people, not always consciously, share interests with other people. Human beings undoubtedly have a corresponding inhibition by nature, although being able to control their instincts they can also control their inhibitions. It is still accepted morality among schoolboys that 'you don't hit someone who is smaller than you', and terrorists may sometimes let women and children go free. Just as the conquered animal appeals to the victor's parental instinct, so the 'weakness for the weak', the most humane feature of human beings, is the mainspring of attempts to control aggression. As the book of Proverbs puts it, 'He that is slow to anger is better than the mighty; and he that ruleth his spirit than he that taketh a city.'

What weakens the instinctive inhibition of human beings is

their ability to use weapons which enable them to kill without coming face to face with or laying hands on their victims. Increasing expansion of the arms industry, in which deranged instincts form a kind of chemical compound with economic interests, means a progressive alienation from nature. The arms race does not merely increase the strength and quantity of armaments, it may also 'reinforce' people in ruthless, aggressive attitudes. It is less than a half-truth to say that 'we have weapons in order not to use them'. Since it is weapons which liberate us from the aggression inhibition, they cannot be the most natural means of combatting aggression. In order to overcome the confusion about aggression, it is necessary to distinguish between four forms of aggression:

1. The first is that which serves the species in its struggle against other species and helps to preserve a balance in nature's vast household between species which are vitally dependent on one another. By developing tools for aggression humans have made themselves the lords of creation and have often pursued their taste for the hunt beyond what is socially and naturally expedient. (The extermination of whales or the wholesale slaughter of African elephants solely to display their tusks as trophies are just two examples of this.) The only threat to human beings now comes from their own species and from those animals which cannot be made into prey for the hunt, namely the insects; and increasing technological interference in nature does nothing to lessen the insect threat. Insecticides have proved to be a two-edged sword, partly because they pollute nature and disturb the natural balance between species, and partly because many insects become resistant to them over just a few generations. We should learn from this that nature is as entitled to 'natural rights' as people.

2. As the 'lord of creation' the human species has turned its weapons and its aggression against itself. The outbreak of war usually arouses wild enthusiasm on the side of the aggressor, there is a fervent spirit of comradeship in arms and a common enemy can help to strengthen solidariy. When arguing that aggressive tendencies are not innate, references are frequently made to tribal groups like the Papuans of New Guinea who display very peaceful behaviour. It becomes clear on close examina-

tion, however, that their children are brought up to vent their anger on objects. What their behaviour shows us, therefore, is not that aggressive tendencies are not innate but that these tendencies can be socially controlled, especially in communities living in extreme isolation. There are also many examples of how neighbouring tribes will mark out their territory simply by use of threatening behaviour or arranged competitions which do not develop into full-scale war. There can be no doubt that aggressive tendencies or the social relations by which they are released have become strongly developed in the great urban civilizations and particularly in the Western world.

Territoriality can still have positive effects when it manifests itself as local patriotism, negative effects as nationalism, although differentiation must be made between nationalistic defence of one's own territory and invasion of others'. Division into territory, or the desire to control one's own area, is so primordial in man that feelings of joint responsibility for the whole must depend on real responsibility for one's own surroundings.

3. Collective aggression may turn not just against other societies but also against society as such. Fighting against an outside enemy can strengthen solidarity but it also makes society more militant. When warfare is motivated by economic interests, conflicts of interest occur in society since it is usually the interests of the ruling class for which everyone is compelled to fight without receiving an equal share of the spoils. Internal tensions are artificially diverted into the struggle against an external enemy, war becomes necessary for peace, and the fight for dominance of the world exacerbates the class struggle. It is a self-perpetuating process which has left its mark on the history of Europe and come to a head in two world wars.

The ideologists of socialism were right to emphasize that the common interests of the lower classes are supra-national; but nationalistic motives have always proved stronger than ideological incentives. Class is far more of an abstract quantity to its members than the nation is to its citizens. To put it another way, economic motives are less elemental than nationalistic motives based on territorial aggressivity.

While war may diminish internal conflicts, peace can make them more acute; and this applies equally in both rich and poor societies – yet further evidence that material progress alone is not enough to counteract aggressive tendencies. Group aggression towards society, collective violence, has become more prevalent in the rich societies where there are no common values over which to cooperate but material values over which to quarrel. In the 1970s group terrorism has contributed to rising aggressivity in several Western societies. In dictatorships, where the state has taken out a patent on violence, terrorism has little chance of success; terrorist pressure is usually directed towards democratic states whose weakness, despite accusations of social violence, lies in the fact that they cannot be as ruthless as the terrorists. So long as terrorists are unable to threaten use of plutonium bombs and the like they will be no more dangerous than the demands for countermeasures which they provoke, demands that democracy should adopt features of totalitarianism. All extreme forms of taking the law into one's own hands threaten the development of democracy and panic measures in its defence merely serve to put democracy at risk.

Anti-social sectionalism is itself evidence of the strength in group solidarity – when it cannot be used positively within society it may turn negatively against it. The group is concrete, society remains abstract as long as its members have no sense of solidarity with the whole. The group (tribe, extended family, etc.) in which everybody knows one another and individuals participate in the whole, was the original social unit and formed the original focus for solidarity, a sense of cohesion which becomes conformity in the anonymous mass society. The kind of mass hysteria in which the individual enthusiastically surrenders his will to the leader is an unhealthy regression to primitive group solidarity, the difference being that the group of independent individuals has turned into an undifferentiated mass.

4. It is collective aggression which once aided the survival of the human species and of the individual tribe or nation: and it is this kind of collective aggression which endangers the individual society and mankind. *Individual violence* is relatively less important although it generally attracts most notice and arouses the greatest indignation. The aggression threshold is lower in the group than in the individual; the coward can be a real dare-devil when he is in the majority. The individual violent criminal is

usually a pathological case; aggression against the immediate family (crimes of passion, child battering, and so on) is a different matter and is usually rooted in frustration, emotional and economic hardship, bad housing and so on.

Those who deny that human beings are born with aggressive tendencies attribute *all* aggression to frustration, and to sexual frustration in particular. Certainly in our culture aggression has often been a kind of substitute for sexual satisfaction. It may be no coincidence that the age of imperialism was also the era of Victorianism, and that optimism about development and its concomitant belief that civilization makes people civilized should have been strongest during that period when the peaceful colonial powers were trying to 'civilize' the savages!

It is collective aggression that is dangerous, but a predisposition towards it is present in the individual. Children of 8-10 months display fear of strange people even when they have had no unpleasant experiences with strangers, slightly older children display active enmity. Both fear and anger reactions are innate and linked to a recognized hatred of strangers known as 'archaic intolerance'. Children do not have to *learn* to fear and despise and ridicule deviations from the norm but must be taught *not* to, and this is one of the major functions of upbringing.

When one considers the overkill of which the world is now capable, aggressive tendencies spell mortal danger. To direct the fighting spirit against aggression is a sensible defence mechanism as long as moral indignation really is being turned against aggressive tendencies and actions, and not against the facts relating to aggression. Just as sex was taboo in the Victorian era, there is now a tendency to consider it improper to regard people as potentially aggressive. Victorianism led to sex on the brain, what will the aggression taboo lead to?

PREVENTION OF AGGRESSION

That which holds true of animals, namely that crowding of territory breaks down natural inhibitions and increases aggressivity, can also be assumed to hold true of people. It is clear at all events that crowding does not increase fellow-feeling, but on the contrary heightens indifference towards one's fellows, an attitude that is further reinforced by what could be called 'institutionalized humanity'. It is easy enough to draw conclusions from this that would radically affect housing policy, but it is more difficult to put them into practice.

Excluding cases where anger is actually vented on the immediate family, what counteracts aggression is personal knowledge of other people and their background, whether they be external enemies, criminals or other deviants from the norm. In times of war fraternization with the enemy is a serious threat to the fighting morale. The mass communications media can both incite people with propaganda and inform them with facts – one argument why the mass media should not be controlled by the rulers.

Since aggressivity is increased in situations of stress, such situations should be avoided. There is evidence that national leaders, who have far too much to do with decision-making about far too many things, are permanently exposed to stress. The best means of preventing aggression within the nation is to give everybody a share in responsibility for the whole, not just technically but in reality. The gap between democratic ideas and social realities is frustrating.

Since incomplete satisfaction of physical and psychological needs leads to frustration, science has an urgent task to explore these needs. Considerable scientific advances have been made in other areas. Medicine has almost eradicated the diseases which were endemic to the poor society, but it has not been able to prevent the diseases which are more common in rich society, and which are in fact partly caused by the nature of society, i.e. by a lifestyle that is wrong. Wrong in this context means unhealthy rather than morally wrong. One of the great humane advances has been the recognition, applied in medicine, that disease is not punishment but unmerited suffering. Even so, the general tendency to remove responsibility from the individual in the mass society has led to a tendency on our part to neglect responsibility for our own health. The morality of the poor society made it virtue to endure suffering; nowadays when analgesics are readily available this has become pointless. The enormous consumption of tranquillizers and stimulants is clear evidence that the natural rhythms of existence have become disjointed in modern life, and that living today is somehow both too tense and too unexciting.

The Danish physician Knud Lundberg has forwarded the hypothesis that 'the basis of the most dangerous diseases in the industrial society – which will kill over half of us – may well lie in the life as onlookers which we are not born to lead.' To take an example, we may have our fighting spirit psychologically stimulated in front of television without being able to work it off in the kind of physical activity our bodies are tuned to expect.

Violence as entertainment, a popular form of family diversion in the unexciting welfare state, is more likely to stimulate the desire to fight than to abreact it, while looking on at others' suffering increases indifference to it. Children in our society are confronted at an early age with the horrors of the world, while their opportunities for self-fulfilment are severely restricted, in the psychological pressure of the city environment if not elsewhere.

If suppression leads to frustration no good will come of suppressing the competitive spirit. But there is a difference between forms of competition; the dividing line can be seen where sporting matches which satisfy physical and psychological needs in the participants, erupt into disorder and trigger off aggression among both participants and spectators. It is not the competitive society that creates the need to compete: that need is present in other societies as well (in the socialist countries elitist and competitive sports are pursued with scientific and nationalistic determination). And while we must reject 'free competition' as the driving principle in society, this does not mean that the spirit of competition has no social justification at all.

FREEDOM AND GOVERNMENT

At the one extreme there is total and totalitarian control of people, organized coercion possibly effected indirectly through biological and technological conditioning. At the other extreme there is the kind of society in which individuals with no inhibitions pursue their own desires in an unrestrained free-for-all which is bound to result in disintegration for any kind of society. Organized coercion is an assault on human nature, but anarchy is not a natural condition: they are both distortions which deny one of two fundamental needs, the need for independence and the need for guidance. Traditionally, of course, obedience is regarded as a greater virtue than independence, political or otherwise, and the problems of government in modern democracy are linked to a reassessment of these two postures. In modern dictatorships people may be imprisoned for their independence; at the Nuremberg trials people were condemned to death for their obedience (although admittedly in relation to bestial orders). In the democracies there are clear trends both towards totalitarianism and towards anarchy; the trend towards disintegration can only be halted by a reasonable balance between freedom and governing concepts which do not need to be antithetical.

The opposite of suppression is not licentiousness but self-control. Unlike animals, human beings are not bound by instinct; those people who are victims of their impulses and act 'in the heat of the moment' are no more free than those who are prevented by an inhumane society from exploiting their potential. Freedom has both psychological and social aspects, and the social expression of psychological self-control is self-government.

Members of primitive society felt that their chief represented rather than directed them. His power was in the nature of a spiritual authority. In some places the chief would be sacrificed for the community when his period of rule expired so that his strength could be reabsorbed into the natural cycle. There is a primitive basis for the stoic, Christian ideal that the greatest shall be the servants of the least. An early form of self-government was also practised in ancient and mediaeval times at the Scandinavian '*ting*' where people could meet to settle their differences (the French word *parlementer*, meaning 'to come to terms' has given us the modern word parliament, just as the Danish tradition has been preserved in the 'folketing', even if only in name). A group, such as a school class, which needs a spokesman or a structure in order to solve some practical problem, will select its representatives directly on the basis of familiarity with personal and professional qualifications, and a real choice is only possible where there is such familiarity.

Human groups tend to contain their own order of precedence, a system which averts internal aggression in the animal herd. Among mafiosi and criminal gangs this pecking order is extremely well-defined and tyrannical. But just as the leader of the animal pack requires other qualities than physical strength (under natural conditions, that is; in zoos the fiercest ape will often force his way to the top), so among humans it is not the tyrant who becomes the leader under natural conditions, i.e. where a free vote can be made on the basis of personal acquaintance.

Admittedly it is impossible to explain away the fact that the greatest tyrants of both ancient and more recent times have been, if not elected, then at least accepted with the greatest enthusiasm. The reason lies not simply in the powers and propaganda of the dictator, but also in that 'need for the strong man' which is keenly felt in situations of social chaos or war. (And the tyrant himself will generally engender such situations if he has not been engendered by them.) The astounding readiness of human beings to obey in extreme situations cannot be interpreted as pure cowardice but must be based on some primitive craving for direction, an infantile need for guidance. The urge towards independence comes later in the development of both race and individual. Freedom of choice, especially when it is not a real but only a formal choice, can be more stressful than freedom from choice: decisions can be more difficult to take than orders. The kind of 'unpopular' decisions that demand great sacrifice on the part of the vast majority of people may be acclaimed when they emanate from a dictator (as we have seen time and time again) whereas they can cause parliaments great difficulties. The alternative to the totalitarian form of government which progressive crises may turn into a social need and which is greeted with compliance by the infantile need for guidance is real joint responsibility.

A common argument against active democracy is that it imposes too many demands on the individual, in particular demands for greater independence, maturity and insight. To a certain extent it is true that human beings are not born for democracy but must be educated for it; but that does not mean that organized coercion of the kind that prevents people's natural development and keeps them in a state of political immaturity is more 'natural'. If human beings are by nature independent creatures, different from all others, their natural need for self-determination will only be recognized in a developed, democratic society. Liberation from a social order protected by the old morality of thrift and obedience leads in its turn to another either-or: either to a real liberation of mankind, or to a repression of the urge towards independence which more acute awareness of democratic rights makes it hard to justify. Consciousness of democratic duties is undeniably less extensive; a feeling of joint responsibility is hardly likely to occur when the right to democratic participation is reduced to a choice between political representatives who have been nominated by other people and who are only felt to be really representative by very few.

TRADITION AND INNOVATION

A radical difference between our type of society and all previous societies is the faster rate of obsolescence and renewal. It was – and possibly still is – natural that authority and experience grow greater with years, but it is now more common for the wisdom of older people to become out of date. 'Respect for age' is not exactly marked among young people. Nevertheless, the average age of people in influential positions is considerably higher than it used to be, not just because average life expectancy has risen but because far greater demands are made upon the young before they are allowed to play a significant part in society. An increasing number of trades and professions now require increasingly lengthy training, and this is not solely because the practice of a profession has become more difficult but also because longer training is a qualification for higher wages. Above all, however, long periods in education are a way of keeping back the young. The school-leaving age has been raised in all industrial societies, in some places to the age of 18, which must surely be a pointless measure.

In a static society where the young have only to carry on the old traditions there is little scope for independent urges – this may have been why young members of many primitive societies had to go through severe trials and ordeals before they could be accepted as adults: something had to be knocked out of them first. But they *were* accepted as adults at a much younger age than young people in modern society where the need for renewal and innovation is much greater. Before the breakthrough of industrialization, children took part in adult work (although admittedly they were abused in many cases), and at adolescence they entered the ranks of the adult. Until the turn of this century puberty does not appear to have been a critical phase, still less a phase of criticism against society. The faster society has developed the longer the period between childhood and adulthood has grown, to the point where youth in modern society is virtually a 'culture' in itself.

As human labour is rationalized away, both children and old people find themselves unable to play a useful role in the life of society; to an increasing extent the youngest and the oldest members of the community are taken care of in institutions. Young people, too, are sent to vast educational institutions which are cut off from the community to form artificial communities in themselves. The job shortage of recent years has particularly affected those young people who have not yet started their working lives. Since inflation, rising land and property prices have also made it increasingly expensive for young people to buy their way into society; it is beginning to look as if the older generations are deliberately consolidating their position vis à vis the younger, while at the same time making youthfulness an ideal.

The fact that the very age group with most energy and enterprise should be kept away from influential positions is the most depressing evidence of the irrationality of modern society, its internal dissension and its waste of resources. What it means is that those people who are destined to renew society are more likely to come into conflict with it, especially now that economic development has undermined the old standards, weakened belief in authority and strengthened the urge to be independent. For the children of the welfare state who are far more used to wealth than the older generation was in its childhood (and who are sometimes envied by the older generation for that reason), the disparity between expectations and reality is even more frustrating and disruptive. It is hard to think of any time in the past when young people rebelled against their own society or culture just because they were young, as they do now, and all this at a time when the culture is less rooted in tradition and less authoritarian than it ever was in the past! It is also worth asking whether, despite its political superstructure, the recent youth movement was not basically just as much a reaction against the lack of tradition and authority as a reaction against prevailing standards and authorities. It is characteristic of industrial civilization that there is a gap between the traditional moral values and what occurs in practice; between the good and the useful. The youth revolution queried the value of the useful, and it is no coincidence that it came to a height during the wave of affluence in the 1960s.

In a society where living conditions are continually changing and standards have lost their power to persuade, the upbringing of children poses problems which did not exist in societies more bound by tradition. In the last 50 years or so the problems of upbringing and schooling have been among the most controversial. Because there is no one accepted set of values, anxieties may arise that children will be indoctrinated into following different ideals from one's own, whether they be 'bourgeois' or 'revolutionary'.

So long as society allows people to hold different opinions, any kind of one-sided indoctrination will be a two-edged sword since human nature, with its independent urge, tends to react against strict discipline. This does not mean that indoctrination should not be condemned: however indoctrination does not consist in one teacher allowing his or her own views to emerge clearly, but in preventing the emergence of other views. School children should not be taught opinions, but the foundations on which they are based. If we seriously believe that society ought to adapt to people (and not the other way about), then we should ensure that child rearing lays greater emphasis on the satisfaction of children's elementary needs than on the propagation of our own opinions. Because human beings *are* a product of nature (and not only of society) the ends to which children can and ought to be reared are limited; because human beings (unlike animals) are shaped by their environment the potential damage caused by an upbringing which disregards the nature of the child is limitless. It is, for example, a fatal mistake to believe that children can be liberated from 'bourgeois individualism' and become social creatures if they are prevented from forming attachments with a single individual, from being themselves or from having things of their own. The acquisitive urge is a natural one. Attachment to objects also occurs in all cultures and it begins very early in the small child. Bourgeois education consists not in teaching the child possessiveness, but in teaching it early on to share things with others. But if one refuses a child the right to possessions on principle, then one produces experiences of frustration. And apart from this material culture is based on this love of things' (I. Eibl Eibesfeldt, *Love and Hate*, p.230). Like free competition (or freedom to put others out of the running) the kind of private ownership which brings the power to exploit others is a distorted development of innate tendencies which will not be removed simply because they are ignored or repressed. On the other hand, ownership of the means of production, of land and housing cannot be justified in terms of the primitive urge to possess. According nature its proper emphasis does not mean allowing a small minority to fulfill all their instinctive impulses, but creating a civilization in which there is a harmonious balance between biological needs and social requirements.

As we have already mentioned, the child needs to form a close attachment to one specific person; it is also true that in its search for its own identity, the child needs models to identify with, and it is this desire to identify which forms a basis for the ability to empathize, the most moral attribute of human beings and the antithesis of blind conformism. A 'free' unbringing which lays down no guide-lines is no more an upbringing for freedom than an authoritarian upbringing: the first leads to fundamental distrust, the second to servility and both these are expressions of psychological constraint.

THE INDIVIDUAL AND THE COMMUNITY:
THE NATURAL RIGHTS

Human beings are by nature social creatures. It is by virtue of the ability to establish differentiated societies that they have subjugated the earth; and the individual is probably given more scope in tribal communities where each person takes a share in the whole than in the mass society where each person may have greater independence but scarcely greater significance for the whole. The meaning of existence is less urgent an issue for those who have their natural place in the community than for isolated individuals in urban civilizations. Where community feeling is slight, the feeling of meaninglessness intrudes.

The meaning of life was originally a social experience. Through communal acts of worship even stronger than solidarity in arms people came to worship those forces which maintain the community and to find ecstatic expression for their own feelings. Originally, in primitive societies, phenomena were interpreted as being animate. This meant that people would project their own souls into nature and interpret themselves as well as nature in myths and symbols which they saw, not as symbols, but as the innermost reality of existence. The biologist Jacques Monod believes that we have inherited the primitive need for meaning and this argument is supported by the fact that when dreaming we interpret our lives in symbols, many of which are related to the symbol world of early myth, and by the fact that our dreaming has both physiological and psychological functions vital for our spiritual health.

This need for meaning underlies all the different religions which have a remarkable amount in common despite their variety and which share the same social function. It is worship and religion which unite the members of society in a fellowship not merely of interest but also of feeling. Originally the values of life and the values of society were perceived as identical; social standards were felt to be rooted in the essence of existence. It is this relationship between the psychic, the social and the religious which disintegrates at times of crisis.

As we have already mentioned, the major critical phase came with the transition to urban civilization which led not simply to economic and national conflicts but also to a crucial and related change in the function of the gods. In primitive societies gods were personifications of natural forces, in urban states they became personifications of the collective powers of the state. The gods became national, war gods occupied a strong position and the state religion acquired a more political function to become a deliberate weapon of control in the hands of the ruling powers. It was during this phase that the old wise men and prophets preached the one supranational god who is common to all people and accessible to human beings without the mediation of society's priests.

Monotheism, the belief in one god, is historically connected with individualism, here taken to be the recognition and acknowledgement that the individual is valuable in himself regardless of social standing. Behind this fundamental humanist perception lies an awareness that individual self-fulfilment is impossible in a society where class and working divisions are more pronounced. It was in opposition to the prevailing social justice (or injustice) that the philosophers formulated the idea of humanity, a concept embracing all people on an equal level, and the notion of natural law which naturally applies to all.

While individualism in this sense may be regarded as one of the great civilizing advances, there has, especially recently, been a tendency partly marxist in origin to regard 'bourgeois individualism' as a phenomenon of social decay, an atomization of society in which the individual pursues only his own ends in competition with everybody else. If this is where a strict adherence to liberal politics leads, however, marxist-leninist politics lead to the total subordination of the individual to the demands of state or party. At times of armed struggle (as for example during the Chinese revolution), such subordination may be appropriate and necessary; but it can no more be a social ideal than liberalist selfishness.

Individualism and collectivism do not need to be antithetical; indeed both selfishness and regimentation are distorted developments of the primitive needs for independence and cooperation. Obviously some people are more individualistic than others, and in a humane society there must clearly be room for the lone wolf. It is the enterprise of the creative talent that leads to scientific breakthrough and artistic innovation, and it is narrow-minded to suppose that individual achievements are not necessary for society, or even that they are antisocial because (as culture with a capital 'C') they give rise to elitism and snobbery. (In China there has been a problem over relations not only with European artists but also with the nation's own cultural elite from Confucius to acrobats and scientists.) The first argument against this view is that scientific and artistic innovation contribute to social innovation, although they cannot be measured in economic terms; the second argument is that the state should not have the right to curtail any form of human activity and self-fulfilment which does not directly harm other people. The fact that artistic and scientific opposition is inconvenient for the state does not mean that it is harmful to society.

Even in a liberal, individual-oriented society there are large numbers of people who feel that their opportunities for self-fulfilment are restricted by their family patterns or working conditions. It is possible to find examples in almost every social group (housewives, wage-earners, school children, etc.). Many people feel that they have potential which is being repressed or underused. The result is often frustration or more severe psychological problems.

111

Over the history of evolution human beings have adapted to small groups of simple structure. Since we cannot go back to nature or return to stone-age tribal society, we have no course but to continue striving for a democracy based on small units in which the individual is not an incidental piece of raw material for the rulers and the technocrats. Our point of departure must be the natural rights of human beings; where these rights are not respected, mass society becomes primitive in a far more threatening sense than primitive society.

– By nature human beings are independent, active creatures, it is therefore against their nature to be reduced to passive objects for others' decisions.
– By nature human beings are individuals, different from all others; it is therefore against their nature to be reduced to members of the herd.

RATIONAL AND IRRATIONAL; SCIENCE AND ART

One difficulty lies in the fact that natural rights are not a concept of natural sciences but of ethics. In our modern society those truths which are binding for all people despite occasional attempts by ideologists to manipulate with them are the objective facts of science; and objectivity is the best defence against all attempts by ideology to reinterpret things from self-interest. But even the scientific attitude tends to overlook anything which cannot be broached in objective concepts. We started this chapter by discussing how behaviour technology tends to disregard everything internal and innate in people and reduce them not even to nature but to mechanics. In this respect science is no longer objective or impartial but determined by interest: an interest that people *are* as they must be if they are to be turned into objects for exhaustive scientific observation – and manipulation.

When one compares the different theories concerning people and society (e.g. behaviourism and psychoanalysis, liberalist and marxist economics, etc.) one must recognize that there is not *one* entirely objective science dealing with these subjects (there may be none at all). It is only by virtue of a totally arbitrary and reductionist view that people and society can be made into 'objective' quantities. Even where objective perception is possible, however, in the natural sciences, objective knowledge contains no guidelines for its own use. There are no objective criteria for the application of objective science; generally speaking encouragement is given to that area of research which serves economic and power-political interest.

Although research into humanistic subjects is neglected in favour of research into the natural sciences, our knowledge of human beings and their needs is sufficient to change the way our society and our world are organized if we put it into practice. But when we say 'we', we immediately identify with the common interests, with humankind which does not exist as such. It is true that humanity has probably never been subject to a common destiny to the extent that it is now, but neither has it ever been so armed against itself. This does not mean that there are no common values still rooted in nature, but it is difficult for these values to stand up against the dominant alliance between 'impartial' science and economic, nationalistic and power-political interests.

The present economic and scientific orientation is characteristic of an industrial society which arose from a politico-economic revolt against the privileges of rank in the old society – and from a scientific rebellion against the mediaeval Christian interpretation of the world which formed the ideology of the old society. The objective perception of an intrinsic connection between things makes it possible, first, to interfere in those things and, consequently, to create a technical civilization. In so doing, however, an intellectual need for causal explanations becomes divorced from the primitive, emotional need for meaning. Science becomes the business of experts who, as it were, divide reality between them into areas of professional competence which often claim to be the whole or basic picture. This degree of specialization can also lead to a split between the intellectual and emotional aspects of human beings. Human beings do not *become* rational because their perception of reality becomes more scientific, simply their irrational, emotional side becomes suppressed.

What was once expressed in the common symbols of religion becomes the matter of art in the industrial society. Until the late 18th century art was in the service of religion and not until this relationship had broken down did artists become conscious of themselves as artists. But when this happened art became more individualistic and the collective symbols became less immediately intelligible in modern art. That art nevertheless has a vital function in modern society is confirmed by the negative attitude to art in dictatorships. It is the repressed which finds expression in art; art has the same function in society as the dream has for the individual – even though he may not remember or understand the symbols of the dream.

Because the tradition of scientific perception was rebellious in its origins, there is an overwhelming tendency in our technical civilization to regard the rational as progressive and the emotional and irrational as conservative, a tendency which has been reinforced by the way male-dominated society underrates traditionally feminine values. It has been considered reactionary to cast doubt upon the blessings of development and to see positive and inviolable values both in nature and in human nature. The outward consequence of this 'rational' attitude is domination by experts, the inward consequence is sickness in the soul – the unsatisfied longing for spiritual meaning appears to lie at the basis of our primitive, superstitious belief in development.

CONCLUSION

Despite all differences of scientific opinion and conflicts of ideology, we do have enough knowledge to establish that there is a disparity between the needs of human beings and the needs of industrial society. The less human beings are able to assert themselves in society the more total becomes the social machinery of control, and vice versa. This trend leads towards the totalitarian state.

It would appear to be a law of history that the great civilizations develop symptoms of disintegration when they are at their zenith. In his book *Decline of the West* Oswald Spengler voiced the opinion that the development of civilization was like an inexorable biological process, a progressive deviation from the natural order. Society, which was originally a natural organism, becomes an artificial, bureaucratic organization.

It is one thing, however, to say that civilization grows sick when it moves too far away from its natural foundations, and quite another to view this kind of historical development as a natural, i.e. biological, process. The madness of development is not the result of progressive insanity in civilized human beings; if anything the converse is true. This naturally raises the question whether the human mentality is so much a product of development that it cannot be changed. Although Karl Marx and his successors may be right in thinking that in the last instance it is the productive forces that determine the nature of society and of spiritual life, they are not right in supposing that the development of the productive forces in itself leads to a better society. Nor are they right in allowing development to determine human needs.

According to Marxist theory, society will reach a point of crisis when technical possibilities can no longer be realized within the economic system. This crisis is a matter of fact. If development in itself resulted in a transition to another system, it would have happened already. That is why Marxist theorists speak of the 'delay of the proletarian revolution'. In reality the incentives for a classic revolution in the wealthy countries are diminished by material progress; social change will be prompted from other motives and they must be sought in the spiritual needs which remain unsatisfied in mass society.

If 'the complete satisfaction of the material and spiritual needs of all members of society' is to be our goal, we must take the recognition of these needs as the point of departure for a determined programme. If we seriously believe that people's varied abilities and natural needs ought to be recognized, then this must imply that:

1. Each person has the right to decide for himself or herself.
2. Each person has the right to participate in decisions concerning his or her environment, work and society as a whole.

This means that:

3. Society must be based on small units with real self-determination.
4. Leaders must be elected on the basis of personal acquaintance by those they represent. Positions of power dependent on inheritance, wealth or economic privilege ought not to exist.
5. The earth and its resources should be common property.

Only when human nature is accorded its proper significance can a society in balance with external nature be created.

CHAPTER FOUR

THE GOAL

In the three preceding chapters we have illustrated the weaknesses of the existing social system in relation to human need. Our analyses point to a series of preconditions which must be fulfilled in a future society if it is to work as a fruitful basis for human activity and fellowship: democratic joint responsibility, personal freedom, economic equality, ecological balance, solidarity with other groups (national and world-wide). We call a community with these fundamental features a humane, ecologically sustainable society.

Different people will use the same fundamental features to build up different pictures of this future society and will pay attention to different aspects of it. It is difficult to create a picture of the whole, but without a functioning whole there is no point in solving the partial problems. In this chapter we shall describe one version of a future society based on the desired features. This will not be a static and definitive solution but a dynamic and experimental society in a state of continual evolution. It is therefore possible to imagine many variants other than the one described here, especially when it comes to organizational detail.

For human and techno-economic reasons, the transition to a humane, sustainable society must not be too abrupt and drastic. For human and ecological reasons, however, the transition should not be deferred for too long. Our picture of the future is therefore set at a period one or two generations later than the present time, i.e. some way into the next century.

Problem solving of this kind is of a dual nature, partly theoretical and partly practical. We can ask: how should society be organized so as to avoid the problems now causing us so many

116

trials and tribulations which do not appear to be soluble within the existing economic system? We shall try to answer this question in this chapter, thus making it a kind of utopian manifesto.

The next question is whether this manifesto can actually be realized. It is possible to point to a number of practical problems, many of which we can formulate ourselves, and these we shall attempt to, if not preclude, then at least anticipate by raising and trying to answer some of the most likely questions. It is possible to criticize both our theoretical pre-conditions and the over-utopian and theoretical aspects of our manifesto. One obvious objection may be that it is impossible to achieve, but then there is the obvious response that present developments cannot continue without serious breakdown. Our basis for this statement should, we hope, have been demonstrated in the previous chapters.

To avoid remaining totally theoretical and utopian we shall try to indicate the route to a more humane society. The final chapter, number 5, will therefore be a kind of political action programme.

The following paragraphs contain an overall picture of our new society. It is within this framework that the subsequent description of day to day activities must be set.

OVERALL PICTURE OF THE
HUMANE, ECOLOGICALLY SUSTAINABLE SOCIETY

People living some way into the 21st century have evolved a number of different family patterns and different forms of production. Individuals have extensive personal freedom to organize their own lives, provided that the basic rules of society are observed. Practical means of safeguarding this personal freedom include the payment of a citizen's wage to every member of the population. The citizen's wages cover basic living costs, so that no one is compelled to take paid work. Anyone wanting a higher material standard of living is ensured the right to a certain amount of paid work.

The bulk of the economy is now run as cooperative enterprises in which all employees exert a democratic influence. These cooperative enterprises are owned by society, but for everyday purposes responsibility is given over to the employees. The overall interests of society are represented on the management board of the business. All employees in the cooperative enterprise receive the same hourly wage.

Although everyone who wants it is guaranteed work, no one has the right to keep the same job throughout his or her life. On the contrary, the aim is that everyone should have the opportunity to work at a variety of jobs, both theoretical and practical in nature. Through the introduction of the citizen's wage, flexible working hours and equal status for work both inside and outside the home, it has been possible to achieve equal opportunities (and duties) for both sexes.

There is no drastic division between work, education and leisure: the aim of all activities is to satisfy human needs. Any job in the community which nobody finds particularly attractive but which needs to be done is dealt with through a form of national service, or in special cases through higher hourly wages.

Apart from the cooperative enterprises, there are a number of small businesses with greater freedom to organize their own structure and wages system, mainly those where the staff is very small (e.g. family holdings, small traders, consultants and many other kinds of small-scale enterprise). In many cases the real hourly wage in such types of enterprise is lower than that in the cooperative enterprises, but small business owners value the chance to organize their own work without having to consider other groups of employees more highly than wages. The institution of severe restrictions on inherited wealth, low interest rates on private assets and a uniform hourly wage has led to far smaller differences in personal fortune and income. Indeed, the new community can now justifiably be called a society of economic equality.

The introduction of economic equality has been a basic precondition for the preservation of the favourable aspects of the market and price mechanisms: these effective distribution mechanisms now function without bias for or against specific social groups. People decide for themselves how they want to spend their income in different forms of consumption, although there may be special taxation on certain products if the overall interests of society demand it. Consumer demand from the citizen is a controlling factor in the manufacturing sector, which means that the complex bureaucracy characteristic of a number of centrally planned production systems is unnecessary. There is no room in the new system for advertising aimed solely at producing artificially increased consumption; this has been replaced by a comprehensive consumer information service.

The market mechanism also governs the field of housing, although land and the majority of houses are owned by the community. Citizens who wish to spend a larger part of their income on housing can lease the most expensive and desirable houses. Levels of rent for older housing stock are adjusted in relation to prices reached at public auctions held at appropriate intervals, while rent for new housing is fixed in relation to production costs. It is possible to order a new house in the local community on this basis. Some people still prefer to save up to build their own houses, although there is no financial advantage in home ownership and no gain for the owner's heirs, whose right to inherit is severely restricted.

Production methods take account of the physical environment and the health of the population. Now, in the early 21st century, only small quantities of oil and natural gas are used for industrial and domestic heating. Solar energy and its equivalents (wind, wave energy, etc.) are the most important energy sources both for heating and for electricity production. New methods of cleaner burning have made coal the most significant supplementary fuel. Coal is also used to a certain extent to make synthetic fuel for cars and aircraft.

Considerable efforts have been made to achieve efficient energy use in all areas of consumption, with the result that gross energy consumption is lower than in the 1970s and problems of pollution from the burning of fossil fuels (oil, coal, natural gas) have been virtually eliminated. A flourishing recycling industry keeps the demand on world mineral resources as low as possible.

Agriculture has increased in economic importance. The majority of people spend some of their working life on farms; many children grow up in natural conditions among fields and animals and not just among machines and streets. There is an emphasis on the manufacture of vegetable products and on production of cheap, healthy foodstuffs for export as well as for domestic consumption. During the environmental crises of the transitional phase there was an increasing demand for such products. The new decentralized research organization has achieved good results in this field.

Political government is divided into three levels, local, municipal and national. The object of this division has been to achieve active local democracy. All decisions are taken as closely as possible to the affected citizens. The civil service has been decentralized and only those decisions affecting the whole country are taken at top level.

The local community is the basic social unit and should in principle be small enough for all its members to be able (though not obliged) to know one another personally. Most local communities are under 1000 strong. Over a lengthy period new residential areas have been arranged in such a way that joint use can be made of technical equipment with the intention of saving labour and materials and avoiding excessive division of labour. Local communities vary widely in structure and *modus operandi* from the cities to the rural districts, though the basic principles are the same. Compared with the 1970s there has been a considerable shift in population away from the cities to smaller urban communities and rural districts. The political authority in the local community is the local assembly which is open to all local inhabitants from the age of 15, who also have a vote in the meetings. Each local assembly sends a representative to the municipal assembly. This representative keeps the local assembly briefed about municipal problems. In addition the local assembly discusses every question of interest to the local community and puts forward proposals to the municipal assembly.

The size of the municipality is determined such that it can be roughly self-supporting in areas of health, education and culture. This means that the municipality runs children's homes, nursing homes, a hospital, an educational centre, small schools and libraries, sports facilities, assembly rooms for citizens' meetings and other places of cultural activity. Each municipality has a number of cooperative businesses, including agricultural production units. The fact that the municipality is self-supporting means that it provides a tangible framework for everyday human activity. On the other hand, the municipality should not be so large that the various institutions and places of work are hard to reach. Because of this efforts have been made to keep the municipalities down to 40-60,000 inhabitants. In this way it has proved possible to include a number of advanced social activities (including research and university level teaching) in the decentralized municipal system. There are, however, a few national undertakings which demand exceptionally high investment in equipment and specially trained staff. Faculties of medicine and engineering, for example, which require advanced experimental laboratories, are state-run.

The municipality is governed by a municipal assembly composed of representatives from each local community in the municipality. Important decisions are only taken after there has been a municipal referendum in which everyone over the age of 15 has a vote. Attached to the municipal assembly is a cultural council composed of representatives from various organizations and associations in the locality who may take independent responsibility for activities in this field.

The municipalities and local communities work together on physical planning and have considerable freedom to determine use of land. State bodies are only involved in particularly extensive developments.

Each municipal assembly elects a representative to the national assembly (parliament) which is composed of these indirectly elected representatives and an equal number of members elected by direct national elections. Side by side with the parliament is a professional assembly composed of representatives from a number of professional societies, educational centres, trade unions, cultural associations, etc. The professional assembly acts as an advisory body to the parliament and sets up expert commissions for the government. It also has control of some state institutes and think-tanks concerned with technology assessment (in connection with proposed legislation), international development, conflict research, etc., and is responsible for arranging public hearings concerning basic social problems.

All important national decisions are made on the basis of referenda. The legislative work of parliament has undergone considerable rationalization and simplification. Parliament now lays down broad political programmes and spends less time on routine and detail than it did in the 1970s; extended debates on basic political issues occupy a prominent place. It is on this basis that the overall framework for the manufacturing and service sectors and their related wage levels are determined. These figures are adjusted twice a year on the strength of results achieved and expected international trade conditions.

Reorganization of parliamentary procedures has made it possible for the citizen to enjoy far greater involvement in the legislative process.

Obviously there are still conflicts of interest. Different professional groups, local communities, municipalities and regions still compete to a certain extent to promote those activities they value the highest. But in contrast to the destructive fights and sectionalism of the 1970s (particularly as regards economic group advantages), the dynamics of these differences in interest are now being used to benefit society as a whole.

A MUNICIPALITY IN THE 21st CENTURY

X-ville with its 40,000 inhabitants is among the smaller municipalities in the country. It does, however, benefit in several ways from collaboration with neighbouring Y-ville which has 60,000 inhabitants. There is some division of labour between the two municipalities as regards advanced education, and commercial cooperation between them is good.

Production in X-ville

Companies in X-ville manufacture a number of different products. Local industry, which was traditionally based on agriculture, horticulture and textiles, has now widened to include manufacture of electronic equipment for a number of automated processes. X-ville has also become a centre for the specialized manufacture of highly insulated building modules with heat exchangers and other installations designed to fully exploit heat energy in housing, all this being controlled by advanced electronic equipment.

These housing systems are produced by the firm Solarbuild. Together with a factory in Y-ville which produces solar heating systems Solarbuild has found a rapidly increasing market for houses heated by renewable energy sources and by using the 'free heat' supplied by everyday domestic activities (cooking, lighting, etc.). This kind of building is a further development of the 'zero-energy' houses in the 1970s.

Solarbuild was started in the early 1980s by a group of young craftsmen who obtained most of their initial capital from the state loan fund for industrial development. The loan fund agreed from the beginning to treat the firm as an organizational experiment.

It was set up as a cooperative enterprise in which seats on the board of directors are divided between employees (50% of seats), the municipality (25%) and the state (25%). X-ville is now divided into 40 local communities and the community in which Solarbuild is situated is entitled to one of the municipal seats on the board. (The cooperative enterprises may refer solely to the municipality provided that the number of employees does not exceed 20).

During its first five years in operation Solarbuild developed forms of work and organization which have become a model for many other manufacturing companies. All 300 employees have the same hourly wage and the same influence over arrangements for everyday work in the firm. The primary task of the board of directors is to look after negotiations with the community, the municipality and the state over long term production plans. Chief among such discussions are questions of new investment in production equipment and improvement of the working environment, consideration for the physical environment of the neighbourhood and for overall national needs and demands regarding product development.

The board passes on any investment proposals to the assembled work force for their assent or amendment. If agreement cannot be reached, the board has the final decision. If a majority of employees are agreed, however, they can appeal against board decisions to an impartial production committee set up by the government. So far no problems of this kind have arisen at Solarbuild, but other companies have had difficulties which could not be resolved internally, particularly in relation to socially based demands for changes in the production mix where the workers were happy to continue doing what they were used to.

Ironically, one of the things that caused a number of problems for Solarbuild was connected with the firm's unusual success. The employees found it hard to accept the new idea that success should not be immediately reflected in the wage packet. But these new social rules are now regarded as quite natural and reasonable.

According to law, the first 15% of profits (calculated in relation to invested capital) must be divided equally between firm, municipality and state, with the next 15% being divided in the proportion 1:2:2. Any surplus over and above this goes entirely to the state. This system discourages short term price policies designed to exploit specific market conditions.

The firm's share of the profits can be used by the employees for improvements and new investment but not for wage increases. Financing for a further expansion above this is a matter for negotiation between the board, the municipality and the state. Financial support is granted by the state on the basis of the firm's productivity and working environment and the importance of its products for society.

Needless to say, not all such firms run at a profit. If the annual figures of a cooperative enterprise show a loss, the municipality and the state will automatically cover it for one year. The board must then commission an analysis of the causes of loss and submit a three-year budget to the municipal industry committee. This budget may well predict a further period of loss lasting several years if it can be justified on grounds of social need. If the committee does not agree with the firm's analysis and pro-posals and refuses to cover it for future loss, the firm can still continue to operate for three years, provided that finance can be obtained by some other method, e.g. by employees accepting reduced wages. No cooperative enterprise, however, may allow its employees to accept reduced wages for more than three years. If sufficiently good figures cannot be achieved within this period, the municipal industry committee has the right to close the business down (any profit made by realizing assets is shared between state and municipality).

A banking system of considerable ramifications still plays a part in the day to day running of business, as it used to before. But as a result of changes in the political system, the whole banking system has been state-controlled, though local branches (municipal banks) exercise considerable freedom in the granting of credit facilities.

Because working conditions in the cooperative enterprises are good, a large majority of people now prefers this kind of industrial organization. In X-ville 75% of the working population is employed in cooperative enterprises. Of the remaining 25% some work in small-scale agriculture, some as small traders and some in the various professional services. In addition, a flourish-ing cultural life has attracted a number of painters, writers and musicians who live on their citizen's wage and on whatever they can earn from their art, although this may be less than the regular wage in the cooperative enterprises.

No tax is payable on wages earned in the cooperative enterprises or on any other income below a 'maximum earnings' level. This level is fixed annually by parliament and corresponds at present to earnings from a 40-hour working week in a cooperative enterprise. Incomes above the maximum level are subject to steeply graduated state taxation. As far as X-ville is concerned only about 50 people out of 40,000 earn over the maximum, including some of the most popular artists and craftsmen. Salaries and fees for professional services are also fixed, with the result that few people have incomes much higher than the national average.

Members of the board of directors in the cooperative enterprises are elected once a year from among the employees and they may be re-elected. Experience at Solarbuild has shown that the average period for which an employee remains on the board is somewhere between three and five years. Once production and investment plans have been laid down for the next period, the board interferes as little as possible in the day-to-day running of the firm. Employees at Solarbuild are divided into groups of 10-20 people who organize their own operations. Discussions about the groups' working programme take place during the daily lunch break. The group also sends a representative to the firm's coordinating committee which meets twice a week, and this committee annually selects three members to take care of day-to-day management in a formal sense (much as the managing directors of private share-holding companies did in earlier days). At Solarbuild it fast became evident that two of the employees had a special talent for management and administration and these two have now been re-elected for over ten years. The third management position has been filled by different people and has functioned to a certain extent as a training post. One of the guiding principles at Solarbuild has been that nobody should get stuck doing one particular job if it can be avoided. This has led to a fruitful interchange between working groups, and all the evidence suggests that any losses resulting from lack of specialized experience in the beginning are offset by unbiased thinking and by experience of working at other types of job.

The average working week at Solarbuild is around 25 hours, with individual variations between 10 and 40 hours. Both co-operative enterprises and public institutions are obliged to take on more workers if the number of job-seekers in the municipality increases. If a corresponding increase in production or services cannot be economically justified, employees who work above average hours will have their working week reduced. This means that available work is shared. If there is a need in the municipality for more labour than is locally available, attempts must be made to attract workers from other areas. On a national basis, parliament ensures that discrepancies between the municipalities do not become too large by laying down guidelines for average working hours based on statistical surveys of the employment situation.

All cooperative enterprises are permitted a 10% deviation from the fixed average in one year. Anything above this figure requires special permission, which is difficult to obtain. Short term variations in employment opportunities, such as seasonal variations, are counterbalanced by temporary jobs in the public service sector. By applying these simple principles, it has been possible to abolish unemployment with a minimum of bureaucracy: nobody now feels that society does not need him or her, and everybody who wants to work has a job.

Like other municipalities, X-ville has its share of jobs which are less desirable chiefly because many people find them too boring or routine. Jobs of this kind occur in both the manufacturing and service sectors, although attempts have been made to reduce their numbers as much as possible.

The problem has been solved by obliging all people between the ages of 15 and 25 to spend a certain amount of time in these jobs (a kind of social national service). This service is administered by the local community and the municipality and where possible individual interests, physical strength, family conditions and personal career plans, are taken into account when these obligatory jobs are allocated. In certain cases the hourly wage rate for particularly unpleasant jobs may be raised. However, the present solution of a national service for all appears to be so widely accepted that special economic incentives may well be phased out.

126

The interplay between education and production

Experience gained from various regional experiments during the 1970s (including attempts to solve youth unemployment) has led to a change in the relationship between education and work. The theoretical bias once noticeable in the education system has been replaced by a greater comprehensiveness and an emphasis on practical and creative work.

Like other cooperative enterprises in X-ville, Solarbuild is involved in the municipal education system. Twenty or so of the firm's employees are chiefly engaged in arranging youth participation in the production process and this involves children from primary school to university level. The aim is that children and young people should spend a considerable proportion of their time on practical work in the community. At one time the suggestion that this idea should apply right down to the youngest classes in school was greeted with ridicule. But the enthusiastic way the young workers at Solarbuild have joined in sorting waste, making boxes for packaging, clearing, cleaning and so on, clearly demonstrates the sound sense of the idea. An early start also enables young people to gain experience of the working environments in different companies.

Older trainees may have much to offer the enterprise in terms of more up-to-date theoretical knowledge and fresh, detached attitudes to production problems.

Young people are given considerable freedom of choice in selecting the places where they will work, though for practical reasons early work experience will be gained within the bounds of the local community. During the course of their education young trainees must spend at least a year in three different forms of activity, of which at least one should be in the agricultural sector. Among the companies there is a certain amount of competition to attract the young, if only because the state grants an extra investment subsidy for each new trainee.

Through careful planning of urban development in X-ville it has been possible to ensure that kindergartens and schools are situated close to places of work. Whereas work, education and leisure were once kept distinctly separate, movements are now being made in the opposite direction. The workers at Solarbuild take advantage of the local school premises, including the playing fields and swimming pool, which are open to the general public.

In the beginning there were many warning voices suggesting that it would be impossible to continue steady production when working relations were so casual. Experienced industrial managers were appalled at the idea of some members of a working group downing tools and going to the swimming pool while others went to play with the children in the kindergarten and yet others took part in language teaching at the municipal education centre. To their surprise, however, firms like Solarbuild have shown not only that such things are possible without total chaos ensuing, but also that efficiency actually increases, while the workers are more contented.

In the interests of historic truth, it should be pointed out that at the start things were not as rosy for all parts of the country. In many places the transitional period was very hard going, particularly in the large, well-established companies where people found it hard to break with tradition. Most of these companies have now been taken over by the younger generation who identify with the ideas behind cooperative enterprise. The structure in the big companies has now broken down, so that they function more like groups of collaborative enterprises, each limited to a maximum size of a few hundred employees. Experience seems to indicate that when the labour force rises over about 300, it is better to set up a new, independent work place with its own board of directors; otherwise the sense of solidarity vanishes and the employees do not know the people in the other working groups. Many people think that even 300 is too high a figure and there is a movement towards smaller cooperative enterprises working together in groups over some common area of manufacture. Similar ideas concerning the creation of autonomous sections and divisions were already current among some of the large industries in the 1970s. At that time, however, the primary motive was to pinpoint economic efficiency in the various divisions and to stimulate greater competitiveness. The new form of collaboration between cooperative enterprises is progressing remarkably smoothly now that concepts of economic profit and competition are no longer the chief controlling factors.

At the same time, the new principles have changed general

attitudes in the manufacturing sector towards ideas of growth; it is no longer an end in itself to ensure steady growth in quantity of output, the aim is rather to improve the working environment and the quality of the product.

Over the last couple of years there have been discussions in Solarbuild about the possibility of dividing into two or three independent firms, though no definite conclusions have yet been reached. Teamwork within the company is good and many workers feel that they have joined together in building up the enterprise. It will probably be some years yet, therefore, before Solarbuild finds a final solution to its growth problems.

Competitiveness in industry

Unlike the traditional capitalist system, cooperative enterprises have shown surprising flexibility in the adoption of advanced, labour-saving technology. The chief reason for this is that choice of new technology is not dictated first and foremost by profit motives but by consideration for workers' welfare. With the political system prevailing in the 1970s, it became increasingly difficult to get new technology accepted because of the resultant structural unemployment. Typical products of such new technology were optical printing methods and word-processing machines. Workers reacted against new technical equipment with strikes and sabotage. The fact that a number of other industrial countries are still beset by these problems has improved the position of our new society on the international market. A reputation as a reliable and stable supplier of quality products has produced tangible results in the form of a positive balance of payments.

The use of computers is an example of how a controversial branch of technology has developed. During the 1970s the spread of computer technology became so extensive that a number of new social problems were created: great vulnerability to strikes and go-slows, fears that centralized personal records might be abused, loss of flexibility in administrative coordination, lack of personal contact for public-service clients, and the rationalizing away of human labour. A general problem was that computerization was treated as a tool of management particularly suited to large scale production and centralized management and control.

These problems have been largely eliminated since the political change. With the establishment of devolved administration and small-scale companies there is much less need for central computer control. Instead computer technology is utilized in a more individual way and forms a natural part of the daily life of most people: schools, education centres, service institutions and businesses have their own small computers and terminals which can be used by individuals and working groups to retrieve the information they need. Most houses also have their own terminal and many have a mini-computer. Where computer technology was previously centralized and management-oriented, it has now become decentralized and people-oriented.

It may be the surprising improvement in the balance of payments in particular that has led several other industrial countries to experiment with imitations of the new manufacturing system over recent years. In many other countries conflict with workers over labour-saving technology and its consequent structural unemployment has reached a level where the threat to political stability makes new political solutions to their problems a necessity in any case.

Ways of living

Apart from the fact that housing policies encourage contact between people (rather than separating them as before) no one pattern of family or collective living is socially preferred. An important means of safeguarding personal freedom in this respect is the citizen's wage paid to every person from birth. For children under 15 the wage covers minimum expenses for a child living as an ordinary family member. All people of 15 and over receive a citizen's wage equivalent to the minimal living costs for one adult living alone. This means that there is no longer any basis for the proprietorial rights over other people previously upheld by the old sexual morality – family relations can now be based solely on sympathy and mutual interests. Economic independence for husband and wife has decreased rather than increased the incidence of divorce, presumably because all members of the family have jobs to do both inside and outside the home and do not therefore need to impose psychological demands on one another. In the old society there was a close link between small enclosed families and large enclosed institutions; generally speaking it was beyond the ability of the small family to cope with a 'problem' child, and it was all too easy for children to become 'problems' in small families. In larger family groups there are always older people to take care of the younger children, and the children have an opportunity to form relationships with the whole range of age groups.

Communal care of and concern over children means that some people feel no desire to bring their 'own' children into the world. Very small children need continuous close contact with one person. The parents (either of them) thus have a duty during the first two years of the child's life to take care of it, and a right to freedom from obligatory work outside the home. When divorce results in one parent moving away, the children usually remain with the original family group. However, the old style nuclear family has not disappeared; far from it. In X-ville about 30% of people still prefer to live in this kind of family structure.

It is no longer necessary to work in order to ensure financial security for one's heirs. Indeed, nobody is allowed to receive special advantages through inherited wealth, although children and members of the extended family may inherit a certain amount of property (up to about the level of one year's wages). Houses and farms are generally owned by the municipality, but the right to their use passes to the tenant's heirs provided they continue to maintain the property and pay a rent (which is partly determined by market forces) to the municipality.

Economic equality between the sexes has helped to break down the old sexual stereotyping, but it has also meant that sexual differences are given scope and recognition in society as a whole and are not confined to different areas of life. Woman's role in society is as active as man's, men have the same domestic duties as women. In the old days boys were brought up from birth to play the man's role and girls the woman's role. The gradual realization by women that they themselves were helping to create problems for their daughters by the way they reared their sons did much to encourage a change in attitude. Raising both boys and girls to be cooperative and helpful, establishing close ties between children and their parents and other adults, and giving children greater financial independence have all led to a situation where the difference between the generations makes a fruitful contribution to society instead of growing into a gap.

Participation in the work and the cultural activities of the community gives children an opportunity to choose their models and teachers, a fundamental need which the mass society with its restricted opportunities for personal contact did little to satisfy. Those children with special ability who may have found it hard to battle through their environment in the unequal society are now better able to fulfil their potential and find the right kind of guidance.

The new society attaches considerable importance to the idea that people are not mere spectators of cultural activities, but that they participate, that children learn to express themselves not just through words but also through their bodies, in music, dance and drama. There is lively competition between communities and municipalities, not just in all kinds of sport, but also in cultural events, music festivals and exhibitions.

Within the local community there is cooperation of various kinds between family groups and neighbourhood groups. A number of services previously provided by public institutions, such as day nurseries, kindergartens, old people's homes, nursing homes and so on, have now been partly taken over by the local community. This means that most small children and old people can remain in their everyday environment if they so wish. Old people no longer feel superfluous but can continue to make a valuable contribution well into their old age in cooperation with the younger generation. When their physical strength finally fails they can be nursed within the local community by people they know instead of being removed to some distant institution.

There are still enough one-family houses left in X-ville from the old days to cater for the needs of the nuclear families. New building has therefore concentrated on collective houses in which one extended family group can make joint use of a single washing-machine, tumble-drier, freezer, computer terminal, windmill, workshop, etc. Collective houses have large kitchens and family rooms where people can eat together and where much of the socializing takes place but provision is also made for individuals and smaller groups who wish to lead their private lives in peace and spend some time relatively separate from the rest of the group. New collective houses therefore contain a number of small apartments with their own kitchens, etc. Since tenancy rights have much the same effect as rights of ownership, people take just as much trouble to maintain and improve their houses as they used to before the political change. In X-ville there has also been a move to ensure that all new collective houses have about 1½ acres of land where the extended family group can grow fruit and vegetables for their own consumption. For practical reasons it is not always possible to site this land directly beside the house, so the allotment system has come back into widespread use.

Not every municipality follows the same housing pattern as X-ville. On the contrary, individual districts aim to maintain those special features which suit their natural surroundings and their industrial structure. Parliament also offers economic incentives for experimentation in new forms of housing.

Population density in the larger towns and cities has been drastically reduced over the last twenty years or so. The numbers of people living in the largest conurbations have fallen to about half the 1970s' figures. Most of the slum areas have been cleared giving the largest cities a more open character and a larger amount of green space.

A devolved judiciary

Democracy; government by the people, is synonymous with self-control by the people, which means that the machinery of control should be as small as possible. The original means of control was morality, an unwritten code of behaviour, offences against which provoked the disapproval of others. In the anonymous mass society where people do not have concern for each other, morality has little influence especially among the young; criminal behaviour is primarily criminality among the young and a product of bad housing conditions in the big cities. Over-cramped family surroundings may lead to psychological stress; crimes of passion are usually committed against close relatives. These forms of criminality will not be controlled by deterrent punishment or by expanding the forces of law and order, but they will be prevented where family conditions and relationships are neither too loose nor too constricted. Human beings have a need to make their own mark in society, to show what they are worth, to be respected and popular; failure may lead in the worst cases to criminal behaviour. People are most likely to be themselves and to control themselves, when they belong to smaller groups. Feelings of responsibility for society as

133

a whole can hardly be expected from people who have no real responsibility for their own immediate environment and who perceive 'society' as an impersonal edifice of power. Since 'justice' does not mean the right of society over its citizens, but the right of citizens to be themselves, local self government is a fundamental pre-requisite for the constitutional state.

Under the new system only organized crime against society as a whole falls within the province of the state police. They do not interfere in the affairs of the local community except when called upon. The local community has its own police and in many places the citizens take it in turns to provide a police service. The local community chooses people to mediate in disputes between citizens when the two parties are unable to reach agreement, and a committee under the local assembly functions as a court. If punishment appears necessary it usually takes the form of some temporary restriction of civil rights. Appeals against sentence may of course be made to courts outside the local community. The guiding principles of law are that:

1. Judges share responsibility for the future fate of the convicted person.
2. Judges pay due attention to the background of the offence but do not try to deprive people of responsibility for their actions and only refer them for treatment or isolation from society if they are a danger to their surroundings.
3. The offender is helped to resume a normal life.

In many local communities there are collective family groups whose members have taken it upon themselves to care for misfits. They include trained professionals who do not act as superior authorities but work on an equal footing with the lay members of the group: a sense of humanity is not a profession but a natural inclination.

Politics at a municipal level

The municipal assembly in X-ville has 40 members, one representative from each local community in the district. The assembly meets regularly in the afternoon of the first Wednesday in every month. All cooperative enterprises and public institutions in the municipality close on that afternoon. When there are controversial matters on the agenda the session may last well into the evening. The meetings are held in the municipal hall and are open to everybody. Generally speaking two hundred or so members of the public attend, but in special cases this figure has risen to over 500. Members of the audience are allowed to offer brief comments and to ask questions of assembly members who respond then and there. The whole session is broadcast by cable TV to the local citizens, but many people still prefer to attend in person. The monthly meetings of the municipal assembly have developed into a kind of social event, and thus stimulated a real sense of local democracy. (This is one of the many subjects about which the futurologists of the 1970s were wrong. They predicted that modern communications media would eventually make direct contact between people superfluous in many forms of education, meetings, entertainment and so on. If anything, the trend has been in the opposite direction.)

One of the controversial matters recently under discussion in the assembly was a proposal to build a large (2 mega watts) windmill on the scenic hill north of the town. Being very windy this spot is an ideal position, but it is also one of the local natural beauty spots and local communities were divided in their views on the matter. After an intense debate lasting several months it was decided by means of a municipal referendum that the windmill should be sited in a place which was less technically perfect but which did not lead to any clash with the natural environment.

The provision of information and day-to-day intercommunication with local citizens is regarded as one of the most important tasks of the municipal assembly. X-ville publishes its own daily local newspaper containing discussion columns and current information about political, industrial and cultural matters of interest to the community. The municipal hall is also used as an information centre and as a meeting place for citizens and their political representatives.

Each local assembly in the municipality meets at least once a month and if it has no suitable facilities within its own locality may use the municipal hall. Some communities also publish their own informal weekly papers.

In recent years the municipality has used cable TV to transmit public inquiries and subcommittee meetings. Despite the fact that discussions on all local matters are completely open, individual communities have sometimes felt that they were poorly informed. In most cases this has been because the local community representative to the municipal assembly has failed to maintain sufficiently active intercommunication with the community. To reduce the possibility of such breakdowns of communication arising, elections are held at yearly intervals and representatives can be replaced in between times. Generally speaking, however, the problem has been the reverse: local community representatives tend to get stuck in office once they have been elected. To create more dynamism in the system a law has therefore been introduced making eight years the maximum period of office for a representative.

The municipal administration handles payment of the citizen's wage to everyone in the district and coordinates cooperative projects in the municipality.

Another of the major tasks of the municipal assembly is to draw up the annual figures for local job requirements and wage costs which must be delivered by 1 August to the national professional assembly where a review of the national situation is drawn up for parliament.

When the system was first introduced a disproportionate amount of time was spent on these annual accounts. The concept of 'work' was taken too literally and scrupulously, and the difference between paid and unpaid work in particular was sharply defined. When childcare, cooking and other forms of housework came to be paid at the same rate as other kinds of work there was evidence of an (unexpectedly) large interest in working in the home, so large in fact that for the good of the economy as a whole new regulations had to be introduced laying down a maximum permitted amount of paid work in the home, dependent on the size and composition of the family. At the moment, nobody can be credited with more than 40 paid hours a week, whether they work inside the home or outside; but many people actually 'work' a great deal more.

With the present relaxed attitude to paid, as opposed to unpaid work, these regulations present no problem. The job requirements of the municipality vary relatively little from year to year, and the annual employment figures are drawn up quite quickly and as a matter of routine. This leaves the assembly free to spend more time on broader based discussions about the kind of further activities that ought to be pursued in their district. In many cases the final decision is made through a municipal referendum. In X-ville the most recent matter put to the vote in this way was whether expansion should be greater in the health or the education service.

Politics at a national level

Since our future society is based on Denmark, where the population is now about 5 million, we envisage a parliament that has 199 members, of whom 100 are indirectly elected as representatives from each municipal assembly, and the remaining 99 are directly elected. While local elections are based purely on a personal vote, candidates for parliament may be elected on a party basis or as independents.

Parliament selects ministers for 4-year periods; ministers are only eligible for re-selection once. The parliament cannot be dissolved between elections and its members can only be re-elected once. Parliament receives guidance from the public through regular referenda held by means of cable TV; one third of the parliament can demand that an issue be decided by referendum.

The old political parties which functioned chiefly to serve different economic interests are no longer very important. The citizens are still free to organize themselves into interest parties across community boundaries, but parties as such are not represented in the local community and municipal assemblies. Local representatives may feel attachment to a party, and the parties in parliament may obtain support from local representatives, but there is no prospect of the latter advocating greater power for the parties.

For a while there were both Women's and Young People's parties, but they have since disbanded because their major demands have been granted. The largest parties in parliament are no longer economic interest parties in the old sense but less rigid associations of people with a common interest in general social questions, such as the Environment Party, the Technology Party and the Party for Developing Nations. Candidates from these parties stand for election on the strength of manifestoes which give priority to various overall policy guidelines while remaining independent in their views on a number of other matters. Apart from the party members, around 40 members of parliament are elected solely on the basis of their personal views and qualifications without being affiliated to any party. With this kind of composition, there is very limited scope in parliament for narrow party manoeuvring.

Under the old party system the electorate were deliberately hoodwinked into assuming that party election manifestoes were an adequate indication of the political action to be expected from party representatives. The lessons learnt from bad experiences under that system have led to the present structure. Now the electorate is actively involved in every aspect of the preparatory work for legislation and takes the ultimate decision on vital political questions through referenda. With these principles in action, attempts to draw up comprehensive and detailed party manifestoes have become superfluous.

The work of parliament is much less rushed than it was in the 1970s when there was a steady stream of Bills and when the many political parties felt obliged to make themselves evident for tactical reasons. Since the major constitutional reorganization of the 1980s, politicians have become very careful to avoid adopting a position of centralized tutelage over the people. Parliament now devotes a major part of its time to debating matters of principle in preparation for well-considered legislation. The parliamentary year opens with a general debate on the state of the nation based on a comprehensive and thorough document submitted by the government. Whereas this particular debate was once the matter of a few days work, it is now allocated a whole month of parliamentary time; and during this period the citizens are invited to make their own contribution by way of comments and proposals to parliament.

Particular efforts are made to get the population at large more actively involved in national and international political problems. Parliament has its own information and library services which work in close collaboration with public libraries all over the country, thereby ensuring that local communities receive up-to-date information about work in the parliamentary subcommittees. At the same time comments and proposals are gathered from individual citizens, communities and education centres so that this material can form part of the work of legislation. It is no longer necessary to be extremely articulate on the public platform in order to make one's views known to parliament.

It is the task of the professional assembly to ensure that the doings of all political committees are entirely open and to help explain published background material in an impartial and easily comprehensible manner, e.g. through public hearings. Thus, during a period of over a year, public hearings have been held on the problems of developing nations and the way in which industrialized countries can accelerate improvements in living standards there. The mass media have worked closely with the professional assembly on this, and there is every reason to believe that within a few months parliament will submit to referendum proposals for considerable increases in aid to developing nations.

The establishment of a professional assembly alongside the parliament has strengthened political activity. The professional assembly plays an important role as a consultative body preparing the ground for debates of principle in parliament. No important matter is discussed in parliament until the professional assembly has published a thorough review on the subject.

At the moment the professional assembly has 200 members drawn from local education centres along with various professional and cultural organizations and societies. Just as the role of the old political parties has undergone a radical change, so too has the part played by the unions. The Trades Union Congress, which exercised considerable political influence in the 1970s (particularly on the general level of wages), now devotes its time solely to professional and educational questions. It had already become clear by the 1980s that the new social structure and new style of production would make the original task of economic pressure groups superfluous. The only reason why it took so long to act on this realization was that there were still large numbers of people in the permanent employ of the union bureaucracy. A number of other trade associations and organizations have also changed character. In the 1980s the engineering unions for example which had fought throughout the previous decade for higher pay for their members and for the introduction of nuclear energy, switched their attention to professional matters and to further education for their members. Techno-political interests found an outlet in the creation of a new political party, the Technology Party. This party has fought in parliament to make the nation a more prominent competitor in various fields of advanced technology. Since it abandoned ideas of nuclear energy and other forms of mammoth technology, the Technology Party has won a good deal of cooperation from other parties in the national assembly; it has proved very beneficial to combine selected forms of advanced technology with the intermediate technology which now dominates national industry.

Every year during the period from August to October the professional assembly deals with one of its most important tasks, an analysis of the municipal figures for employment needs and wage costs. A comparison is made between statements submitted by the municipalities and information provided by the national office of statistics about the general economic situation – including the exchange balance and market trends as they affect exports. The professional assembly uses this material to draw up a set of figures for parliament with proposals for average weekly working hours and hourly wages (over and above the citizen's wage). After examining the situation in individual municipalities, the professional assembly also makes recommendations about the distribution of state investment and state support for wages according to need. If the cooperative enterprises in a particular municipality have been exceptionally hard hit by international competition, dispensation may be granted for a lower hourly wage than the national average to be paid for a period of up to three years. If the employment situation does not improve during this period some of the local inhabitants will have to look for jobs in other municipalities. Generally speaking, however, problems of this kind have been solved fairly rapidly by increased state activity in the affected municipalities, among other measures.

In conjunction with the employment figures the professional assembly also analyzes the production plans submitted by the cooperative enterprises, relating them to the needs of society and to overall questions of resources and environment. The assembly then proposes outline plans for the following year's production which may well differ from the plans submitted by the cooperative enterprises on a number of points. On the whole the professional assembly has tended to favour a lower growth rate for production than that suggested by individual municipalities, especially when it comes to products requiring large amounts of natural resources. To a certain extent the disparity has been reduced by more extended use of recycling.

The production framework laid down by the professional assembly is not intended to be a means of detailed control over manufacturing in the individual company but a general guideline which state representatives on the cooperative enterprise board will endeavour to promote in future planning. These representatives can exert a special influence in relation to the state contribution to new investment. So far, this flexible form of interaction has proved an adequate means of safeguarding the overall needs of society. The employment and production plans drawn up by the professional assembly are passed on to parliament on 1 October and are so carefully prepared that it is possible for parliament to establish its definitive guidelines within three weeks. Round about 1 May the professional assembly submits a further analysis based on results achieved during the first quarter of the year. As a general rule these supplementary analyses result in parliament making minor adjustments to the guidelines laid down on 1 June.

The people are now so used to the system that they regard it as quite normal that the hourly wage may also be reduced when the figures are adjusted every six months. Only once has the adjustment amounted to more than 3%.

A constructive balance has been achieved between the trends towards centralization and devolution which were once considered opposites and which were rooted in society's need for effective government and the citizens' need for self-determination respectively. In the new system we have a society of societies, a community of communities. Only those social tasks which really belong to the field of national and foreign politics are now referred to parliament and the state institutions.

Security policy

The late 1980s saw a total reassessment of the traditional idea that the nation's continued existence must rely on steadily increasing military defence – in military alliance with the Western superpowers. Independent analysis had shown that the arms race would lead sooner or later to a nuclear holocaust, and in this context further expansion of defence systems along traditional lines began to look totally absurd. Instead the politicians began to seriously contemplate the old ideas about some form of non-violent defence. Arguments supporting the application of non-violent principles were based on two points: first, that use of violence is unacceptable on moral grounds, and second, that war in the nuclear age is totally pointless.

Experience had shown that non-violent defence is not synonymous with defeatism and apathy. On the contrary, defence of this kind can be much more effective than a military machine which is likely to be rapidly immobilized in the event of external attack. The aim of non-violent defence is to influence the will of the suppressor and to prevent him from achieving his ends. Various methods can be used and prepared for, including a refusal to obey the enemy's orders, obstruction of his actions, defiance of his threats and penalties, attempts to break down morale among enemy troops and subordinates, and the creation of a parallel government. With increasing acceptance of these principles, the defence system has come to concentrate its efforts on providing civil guards, services designed to aid navigation and fishery control and to prevent violations of neutrality etc. By this means the basic defence budget has been cut to nearly one quarter of the 1970s figure. A considerable part of the money saved is now used for widely based security purposes: increased aid to developing countries, funding for international conflict research and for international institutions working to promote disarmament and prevent military conflict, and more active representation in such institutions. In contrast to earlier days, the country now sends sizeable and well-briefed delegations to international assemblies and conferences. Delegation members are selected on the basis of their professional and political expertise and a considerable effort is made to provide them with exhaustive and detailed background material. Achievements in this field have produced great dividends: although ours is a small country without much power, our ideas receive a much wider hearing in the international context.

A national initiative proposing the establishment of an international council for conflict research came to fruition during the 1980s with a membership of about 50 prominent personalities from all parts of the world representing different ideologies, races, regions and professions. For the first five years the national government paid for the running costs of the council although it is now financed on an international basis. A group of people enjoying great professional prestige has been employed by the council to provide information about those problems which threaten world peace. The fact that the council has no national axe to grind and is of such a high professional level means that its recommendations have an essential influence on international discussions between the political leaders.

The large savings on national military expenditure have made it easier to win approval for a considerable increase in financial support to developing countries. At the same time there has been a change in the nature of aid so that it has come to be much more like cooperation. Large numbers of young people travel out to the developing countries where they spend a number of years working specifically to introduce intermediate technology to the poorest rural districts. Increased familiarity with the problems of developing nations has led to a new feeling of joint responsibility among the people.

International relations

During the 1980s it became clear that many ideas about closer political and economic integration among the EEC countries were unrealistic. Britain and France had been alternately hot and cold (depending on the special benefits they thought they could attain), Denmark and Ireland were sceptical and vacillating, Italy spent most of its time trying to deal with its own problems. When the situation finally reached a point where only West Germany was still advocating ideas along the lines of political and economic union, the course of the EEC was modified.

Instead of integration the new aim was a looser form of collaboration with an effective supra-national authority over those few areas where it was really needed (use of the seas, certain environmental questions, etc.), while most other areas were dealt with through devolved and less rigid cooperation between nations.

By the turn of the century Norway, Sweden, Switzerland, Spain, Portugal and Greece had all become fully involved in this Western European association. Most goods are free from any trade restrictions, although it has been agreed that there are basic sectors (foodstuffs, energy and certain manufactured goods) in which individual countries or groups of neighbouring countries may wish to become as self-reliant as possible by giving certain trade advantages to domestic products. Denmark, Norway and Sweden constitute such a group within Western Europe and enjoy particularly close political and economic collaboration. (Experience has proved that being 'self-reliant' is not the same as being self-sufficient.)

Ties with the other Western European nations have done nothing to impede the political change at home. On the contrary, our experiments have been greeted with widespread sympathy and followed with interest, particularly by the other small nations in Western Europe. Now that there is evidence that the political change has actually given the nation a competitive edge, interest has further increased; several countries have begun to imitate the new production system and its political ideas.

The most serious opposition to this trend has come from the multinational companies which based their growth to a large extent on division of labour throughout the world and on total economic freedom. They maintained that restrictions on capital transfers and location of production would have a disastrous effect on productivity in general, and that this would harm both the industrial and the developing countries. Practical experience in the 1980s, however, has proved this line of argument to be less than convincing, and over the past 20 years or so the influence of the multinational companies has dwindled.

Having solved their own internal problems, the small Western European nations (headed by Denmark, Norway, Sweden, Holland and Switzerland) have made a considerable contribution towards solving the two dominant problems affecting the international scene: the need for a new, just world order and the need for real military detente. By pursuing an active foreign policy, this group of nations has managed to win a sympathetic hearing in so many countries that real pressure has been brought to bear on the three superpowers. It is still too soon to predict whether the universal holocaust can actually be averted. So far the rich nations have agreed to a sharp increase in economic equalization on a worldwide scale, and the superpowers have accepted real international control of their military sectors.

Perhaps most importantly of all, however, the shift in attitudes characteristic of the political change in Denmark is gradually beginning to spread to an international context.

THE GOAL

We have had to leave many questions about the humane, ecologically sustainable society unanswered and many points have not been touched upon at all. But at this point a moderate sceptic has very conveniently appeared to give the authors an opportunity of adding to their picture of the new society through his (well-chosen) questions.

DIALOGUE WITH A SCEPTIC

A: Quite apart from how well or how badly your new society functions, it is hard to see how it could have developed from the old society by democratic means.

B: Democracy can only be developed by democratic means, not by violence and power.

A: But this presupposes that those in power will voluntarily relinquish that power, which they rarely, if ever, do. The political parties, for example, would have had to decide that political life should not be ruled by parties.

B: All things considered, the idea that a majority in parliament might want greater power for parliament and more say for individual members is not very remarkable. It became clear to more and more politicians that the people's waning confidence in them might endanger democracy. The feeling that those who are elected by the people truly represent the people has changed attitudes towards politicians: they now inspire much greater confidence and respect than before.

A: I find it hard to believe that a change in the electoral system changes anything conclusively. The same kind of people continue to become politicians. Local elections may form a more important part of the overall picture, but it will still be the articulate and the ambitious who stand for election. The rest have neither the oratorical talent nor the desire.

B: There is nothing wrong with being articulate or self-assertive. Local elections however, are based less on electioneering and political wrangling than on the kind of selection processes implicit in daily life. It has become harder to push oneself forward, easier to push forward those who enjoy a great deal of respect. And the constituency is as large, or as small, as it needs to be so that people can keep up personal contact with local representatives. The less articulate and more reticent

145

do not need to take the public stage but can use the local representative as a middleman, much as the chairman of the parish council might have been in earlier days.

A: It is, in fact, possible to over-emphasize the importance of local affairs. The danger of making parliament a super-structure above the local and municipal assemblies is that it then becomes a forum for wrangling between local interest groups which will eventually overshadow the common problems. If parliament is to maintain adequate control over things then local self-determination becomes more a techni-cality than a reality, and local and municipal representatives turn into party spokesmen.

B: What you are saying is that effective government is not pos-sible unless everything is ruled from above. We are saying the opposite: parliament can only deal with the large, common problems if it is free of all the small ones. Small problems tend to grow larger the higher the level at which they are handled. On the other hand, there is, or ought to be, a coherent relationship between local and national (or for that matter international) problems, and the right way to gain insight into larger issues is by starting with the smaller.

A: But the fear then arises that limitations on the power of the political parties might serve to neutralize the real conflicts of interest in society.

B: The fact that you can express *that* as a fear and can also be afraid that local self-government is no more than a technical-ity simply underlines the importance of creating a balance between local interests and other interests. A pre-condition for the equitable society is that political life should not be dominated by *economic* conflicts of interest: at a certain level of affluence economic conflicts of interest become an obstacle to social progress. There is evidence of this in party-dominated parliaments where block politics are practised, but in such a superficial way that no new policies will arise from a change in government. Our system does not have two or three rigid political blocks but a whole range of different people with different views, and this presumably describes the 'pluralist' system to which most democratic parties subscribe in their manifestoes.

A: I doubt whether economic conflicts of interest can simply be eliminated; certainly there can be no doubt whatever that economic freedom cannot be restricted without a large number of control measures. Experience shows that organized control over one sector of society tends to spread to others, in the form of a growing bureaucracy.

B: If anything the reverse is true: it was because the economic conflicts of interest in the old society had made it so difficult to govern that the machinery of government had to grow. If the economy is under control the machinery can be reduced to a minimum. All company figures are now completely open to the public; debit and credit payments are made through credit cards and automatically registered in the municipal banks and the national bank. Decentralization of the public administration has made central data banks superfluous: it is the economy that is governed and not the citizens. Public ownership of land and a direct public share in company profits have led to a drastic pruning of the taxation bureaucracy as well, and removed the source of annoyance which the tax system once represented.

A: It is difficult to ignore the fact that other industrial societies are differently organized from your economically equitable society and that they offer the individual better opportunities of earning money and amassing wealth. You may find that you will have to stop your citizens from leaving the country and build a wall across the border.

B: We may find that we have to deal with an influx rather than an exodus! Our citizens are allowed to travel abroad and settle there but they are not allowed to take out assets they have acquired through the productive efforts of other people and with the underlying support of the nation. The maximum amount that people are allowed to take out of the country is equivalent to the amount they are allowed to leave to their heirs, i.e. about one year's earnings. If differences in earnings potential had any real influence on the desire to emigrate there would previously have been a large migration from the poor EEC countries to the rich. This has not happened, probably because personal and cultural ties are stronger than greed. You think that the greed for wealth will be denied any scope in our society – but why should we assume that it will need any scope? Why should people emigrate to societies

147

where they can earn more – and more, and where no one can get enough and everyone is dissatisfied?

A: Because a society without continued economic growth will grind to a halt and fall behind. You actually receive your citizen's wage for *not* doing anything; you will provide for people economically while weakening their incentive to provide for themselves. This cannot work in the long run. Perhaps the equitable society will be sustained by a pioneering spirit in its early days; but once it is established economic and spiritual stagnation will set in. You are putting a tight curb on growth and preventing people from earning more than anyone else; it may sound very democratic but what it actually means is that nobody is allowed to *be* more than anyone else. The mutual control of behaviour you call morality can also be described as group pressure or 'the law of mediocrity': you must not think you are more than us, you must not think you know more than us. In small communities there is no room for anyone who is a little above the rest, and the greater minds have always turned to the cities. In the Romantic era 'the streets of Copenhagen swarmed with people of genius', many of them came from the country where they were too outlandish to be tolerated. Village gossip is as old as the hills!

B: Exactly, old is what it is! Village gossip is a phenomenon of small communities with narrow standards and limited opportunities for self-fulfilment where everyone knows everything about everyone else and yet keeps themselves to themselves: it is a sign of an unsatisfied need for contact. If people have no business in common then the intimate community is no better than the more distant community, or than the big city where it is easier to stand on one's own two feet. When the eccentrics turned to the capital it was simply because all the cultural institutions were gathered there. Now they are scattered among municipalities which are little smaller in terms of average population than Copenhagen in the Romantic era. Village life in the old days also produced the concept of the local 'character', a reminder that tolerance of misfits was greater in small communities than in urban society where they are institutionalized.

The law of mediocrity is not a law of nature; on the contrary, an order of precedence tends to establish itself in every group of fellow workers. But in the close community it takes the form not of one rigid pecking order but of changing and dynamic associations in which no one needs to feel less important and in which leaders are, so to speak, elected through a long selection process. When people are not motivated to progress for purely economic reasons, their human qualities emerge more clearly and there is more scope for the talents that serve social innovation.

In any case artists have never been particularly motivated by the desire for economic gain. In earlier social systems they found it hard to manage without financial support from patrons or the state and yet they lived for their art. (In our society they are not obliged to live from their work and do not therefore require special economic support.) We can all see that children have the same original urge to express themselves; when society is arranged to promote optimum self-fulfilment rather than maximum earnings this urge need not be wasted.

A: Apart from the fact that it is impossible to live on self-expression, the relationship between artists and society has never been idyllic. All innovation comes from outsiders, new ideas and new art are formulated in opposition to society. Most of the great artists have been solitary figures who would be miserable in your society. Art there will be more like dillettantist self-glorification. It is a fact that in dictatorships where economic freedom is suppressed, free speech and artistic freedom have also been suppressed.

B: In other dictatorships freedom of every kind is suppressed, except the freedom of big business. There is not necessarily a connection. It is a fact, however, that people living in societies where the greed for wealth has not become the social driving force have achieved a more profound knowledge of self and of the symbols of dreams, art and religion than modern Western man. It is only in Western materialist civilization that you have psychologists suggesting a relationship between art and neurosis, as if self-expression were a pathological process. The fact that a great deal of art has emerged in opposition to society does not mean that repression is actually essential to creative art. In a society without repression, art will come

149

closer to resuming its original function. Art has always sought to preserve contact with the hidden depths in human beings, to express those things which can only be expressed with difficulty in social life. The artistic process cannot be reduced to a mere effort to beautify the commonplace and celebrate the positive values of society – there has been no new flowering of patriotic songs in our society. Social liberation implies psychic liberation of the emotional potential that was repressed and belittled in the materialist society. There the unsatisfied need for meaning was exploited by a commercial entertainment industry. Young people in particular were induced to seek a path towards greater perception and depth of feeling through LSD and other drugs. And the need for meaning led to the propagation of salvationist doctrines, to guru worship and so on. Human beings have a primordial need to feel contact with the innermost forces of life – it is this need that has been exploited whenever religion has been perverted into repression or when the state and its rulers have become objects of worship. People are more than products of society, and the most important social function of art is to point the way to this more comprehensive view of human beings. However, it is still up to the individual to seek his or her own path, there are no laws restricting the practice of any creed and a few of our local communities are very much like religious communities.

A: It strikes me that your society consists of nothing but saints! People may have a need for meaning but they also have a need for power and possessions. You can limit rights to property and decentralize power as much as you like, but there will still be people ready to exploit the loop holes and grab as much as they can. Unless of course you care to argue that you have created a wholly new kind of human being – and that would certainly require ruthless regimentation and indoctrination.

B: 'Exdoctrination' may be more what we need. In a poor society where there is not enough to go round, it may seem natural to fight over goods. If the fight carries on into a rich society, does this mean that it is natural for people to seek power and possessions at others' expense, or merely that they are still influenced by social, or rather antisocial, attitudes which are no longer based on economic reality? The fact that rich societies have found it hard to manage the transition to an equitable society is due to their having made competition for financial gain and social position a guiding principle. But is it a law of nature that society must be divided against itself, that some people must be worse off so that others can be better off? Does experience not show, rather, that living well at others' expense is bound to scar the soul, and the soul of society as a whole? Surely a social system which attaches importance to solidarity and not to internal conflict will create a basis for a greater sense of common humanity. Is it so naive to believe that people are by nature social creatures and that if human society departs too far from the natural order it will become inhuman? Or is there really no basis for this belief in practice?

A: Everyone has his or her own belief about the way to salvation, and there is something redeeming in all these beliefs.

B: Let us hope, then, that our belief is justified, but nothing will be achieved without effort. People's attitudes may be influenced by their social conditions, but social conditions are also influenced by attitudes. It must surely be better to believe in human possibilities than in the impossibility of changing anything at all for the better.

A: You have to have the last word!

B: We are still a long way from the last word!

CHAPTER FIVE

THE MEANS TO THE END

It has taken us a large part of this book to arrive at our long term goal in the form of the humane, ecologically sustainable society. The simplest thing would be to stop here and leave it to experienced politicians to find the necessary means to realize the end. There is a danger, however, that the experienced politicians will continue to be so busy bringing their practical experience to bear on problems of the moment that they never have time to spend on the possible means to the end. It may therefore be necessary for us to spell out the first move and to suggest possible intermediate measures.

It is quite feasible that some readers will see this first move as a political programme and that criticism of the technical detail will divert attention from the main lines of our argument. But this possibility is surely preferable to the risk that a convenient shroud of silence will fall over the long term goal because we never suggested the means by which it might get off the ground.

FROM HERE TO THE HUMANE, SUSTAINABLE SOCIETY

There is no need for a revolution. There is need for peaceful evolution leading systematically towards the goal. The long term goal described in Chapter IV includes economic equality, personal freedom, a healthy environment and solidarity in solving social problems. The realization of this goal will entail major changes which will affect the powerful groups in present society. And unless the political remedies are wisely applied these groups will strike again. The fight may be so violent that many people will consider the benefits won too paltry in relation to the pain of the cure. The chief means of winning acceptance for the unpleasant side effects of the transitional phase is a carefully thought-out plan stretching over a long period of time. People can often accept changes when they are introduced sufficiently slowly. Most people, on the other hand, will oppose a rapid encroachment on their well-earned rights.

If we are to exploit fully the possibilities inherent in slow and steady evolution, then we must also be aware of the possibility that other people will try equally consistently to block the evolutionary programme, by procrastination for example. The measures employed must ensure that a gradual pace of change is not taken as an excuse to do nothing. Every point in the political programme must therefore be directed towards the end in view. Some of the proposals in this chapter refer to Denmark, but other Western industrial nations, both large and small, need to consider similar changes if they are to find democratic solutions to their problems.

THE MEANS TO ECONOMIC EQUALIZATION

Economic equality is not an end in itself. But it is a necessary means to the end. The overall aim over the next 25 years must be to level out economic differences in income and wealth among adult citizens in society. This will particularly affect those now aged between 25 and 45. Few people younger than this earn high wages or own great fortunes as yet, and those who are older will be pensioners in 25 years.

The simplest system for levelling out wage differentials is the introduction of the same wage for full-time employment in both private and public sectors regardless of the nature of the job.

This is a break with the principle of supply and demand. As we have already mentioned, one of the chief results of following that principle has been that the most interesting, challenging and varied jobs are usually the highest paid (as with doctors, dentists, engineers, executives of many kinds, and so on). There can hardly be many people who seriously believe that it would be difficult to get these jobs done even if the 'burden of responsibility' were not rewarded through extra high wages. All the evidence suggests that there are enough citizens in the community willing and able to take on the more responsible and challenging jobs for the same wage as is paid for more routine work; quite apart from the fact that in the society of planned equality, as we have described it, work will be more varied. The problems connected with the transitional phase lie elsewhere. In practical terms the difficulty arises from those groups which have already grabbed both the nice jobs and the high wages. These groups will struggle hard to keep what they regard as their well-earned rights. If a great tussle is to be avoided a long term plan will have to be employed allowing for controlled economic development for the different wage groups. However, there is no avoiding basic and fundamental changes in the existing wage mechanism. The following outline offers one example of a *possible* wages policy:

1. Every year parliament fixes the amount by which wages may rise for *those earning less than the national average*. This figure should be set as high as possible allowing for the state of the national economy, although the net result must always be an increase in real wages of at least 5% for this group as a whole. In addition parliament lays down a fixed supplementary allowance to be paid to all wage-earners as (part) compensation for inflation. In periods of adverse economic trends, the supplementary allowance may be dropped and replaced by a framework of *wage reductions for those earning above the national average*.

2. No one earning more than the national average will be permitted any increase in wages other than the supplementary allowance for inflation. No one will be allowed to start earning more than the national average by moving to a new job.

3. Those earning least in relation to the average receive the greatest wage increases and if there is to be a reduction in wages for those earning more than the average the highest paid receive the largest reductions. Details of how increases are to be allocated within the basic framework are worked out in negotiations between employers and employees.

4. No deviation from the given framework is permitted during the course of the year, though in special cases the government may change the way wages are allocated.

This system will obviously encroach on the rights enjoyed by both sides of the job market, but then society does not exist for the sake of employers' confederations or trade unions. If traditional economic growth returns and continues for the rest of this century, wage levelling along these lines could proceed systematically without any drastic reduction in real earnings for those in the top bracket. If there is less economic growth, there may have to be a more rapid decrease in real wages for the highest paid, depending on the rate of inflation. Either way, the rate of change will be gradual enough to allow the individual to plan his finances.

EQUALIZING INCOME
IN THE PROFESSIONAL SECTOR

The combination of interesting work and high wages is neither reasonable nor necessary. As we all know, wages form only part of the total income of the population. A further share comes from professional fees and from the interest and profit on private capital. Although these account for a minor proportion of total income (around 13% of Danes are now registered as self-employed), they do have a considerable theoretical and political (psychological) significance. Equalization in these areas requires further breaks with liberalist principles. The problem of equalization for the self-employed is made somewhat easier by the fact that a large part of this group lie on or under the national average income level. These are the smallholders, small traders and the like. As the owners of small businesses see it, compensation for their comparatively low hourly wages comes in the form of a certain freedom to organize their own working conditions without having to make concessions to management, a large staff, or trade unions. There must also be room for these individualists in our future society, provided that they do not use their efforts to restrict the personal freedom of others either directly or indirectly (as through investing in other enterprises).

The remainder of the group consists of highly paid professional people such as doctors, dentists, lawyers, engineering and architectural consultants, accountants, stock-brokers, etc. Several of these are already more or less dependent on agreements with the public sector. The fact that they have nevertheless acquired incomes well above the national average is mostly due to skilful dealings by their professional organizations and, in some cases, to the fact that they can open negotiations from a favourable position. Imagine the psychological effect of a strike threat from the doctors. It is, of course, absurd that the strike, which was originally the weapon of the lowest paid, should now be accepted as a weapon for the highest paid. The way to combat this is a change in the law: the statutory right to strike over pay should be awarded only to those earning less than the national average. Any highly paid professional group which refused to accept this would have to be nationalized. In any case, this whole question relates only to relatively small groups, and the fact that hospital doctors, for example, are already public employees no longer seems remarkable. Indeed, the commonly held idea that employment in the public sector automatically produces less will to work would appear inapplicable to hospital doctors. The incompetent way in which some countries have bureaucratized former professions only goes to show that more skill is required in introducing changes of this kind. Most arguments against such changes are no more than a thinly veiled defence of the historic advantages of class and cast a slur on those people and organizations which use alarmist methods of this kind to defend their privileges.

During the transitional phase there is much to be said for allowing the highly paid professions to continue organizing their own working conditions. The equalization strategy will involve scaling down full-time earnings for these groups so that they end up around the national average in 25 years. One way to do this would be by making running adjustments to the upper limits for professional fees.

When it comes to levelling out earnings for managerial staff employed in the private sector, salaries could be scaled down by law over the 25 year period. This will most directly affect people who have already reached management level but are not due to retire within the next 20 years or so. For new appointments to management positions there will have to be an earnings ceiling which can be adjusted downwards over the years. The widely voiced threat that this would lead the more enterprising members of our industrial management to look for greener pastures abroad can be anticipated without much fear. For one thing, there are very few 'enterprising' executives so brilliant that foreign countries are straining at the leash to have them; for another, mobility at this level is known to be hampered by national distinctions, (this is less true at lower technical levels). Finally, there is no reason to suppose that there will not be sufficient business brains in the future who regard the challenge of developing the manufacturing sector in a society based on solidarity as more important than earnings. There are already signs of a change in attitude in this regard, particularly among younger people. The chief problem lies in overcoming the transitional barriers. Here, as in other earnings-related areas, the answer may be to use long term, systematic scaling down, implemented at a gradual pace.

INHERITED WEALTH

Financial advantage through inherited wealth must be abolished. In the society of economic equality there will be strict limitations on opportunities to inherit, and these restrictive measures must form a basic element of the political programme. Without the chance to inherit, the relatively small group of people who now enjoy enormous wealth and the unearned income derived from it will gradually disappear from the social system over a generation or so. Private assets will be transferred to public ownership, e.g. in the form of cooperative enterprises. One way to promote economic equalization is thus to introduce stringent laws relating to inheritance, so that any part of an estate valued at more than a certain maximum amount (an average annual income, say) is taken over by the public sector. The great majority of people will be no more affected by this than they are by existing laws, since their share of the estate will be within the proposed limits. Valuations of goods and chattels, such as furniture, should of course be kept reasonably low as they are now.

Particularly valuable assets (such as works of art) will have to be treated differently. Existing estate duties already create

157

problems for people who inherit property of this kind. However, a society in which economic freedom is not prized above all else has a fresh chance to consider human interests in such cases. Gentle changes could be introduced by awarding heirs the custody of works of art and obliging them to be responsible for maintenance, where this does not appear to conflict with the better social use of such assets. The important thing is that works of art will then be owned by the public, so that no legatee can sell them to create extra income inconsistent with the objectives of economic equalization. Future generations will have grown used to the idea that nobody can secure special rights to works of art simply by inheriting them. People will either have to save to buy them, or share their enjoyment of them with others.

One of the special problems of the present Western economic system is that disproportionately large capital gains may be allowed to accrue through appreciation in the value of land and property. Despite much talk of doing something about the economic inequalities that arise in this way, no government has yet been able to take effective measures against them. Given the overall aim of public ownership of land and property, a quick method would obviously be to change the law so that all appreciation in value, after adjustments for inflation, was transferred to the state, e.g. in the form of a public mortgage on the property. In order to alleviate the economic effects of this on the present owners, interest payments on the public mortgage could be deferred for ten years or until such time as the property changes hands. On selling the owner should be obliged to offer the state his property at valuation price.

Instead of selling municipal land to private property developers and builders the municipality should retain ownership. This would offer a better chance of developing types of housing adapted to the needs of the future and to the special nature of the municipality. It would also enable preparations to be made for general ownership of land and housing by society.

There are also good reasons for adjusting the system of progressive or graduated income tax which has tended to become less and less progressive; the extent to which the system levels out incomes at the top end of the scale is now all too modest. Similar criticisms can be levelled at tax allowances which are of greater benefit to the highest paid than to anyone else.

Recently the need for an incomes policy has been the subject of much debate. At the same time we have seen that such a policy is not politically possible because no groups of wage earners are prepared to moderate their claims – to benefit other groups. An incomes policy is only realistic as one element in an integrated programme of social action which aims to achieve an agreed end. In this sense, the equalization scheme we have described might well be called an incomes policy.

THE DEVELOPMENT OF A
NEW PRODUCTION STRUCTURE

Society must support experiments in alternative production structures – instead of putting obstacles in their way. At the moment experiments in alternative production structures are being conducted in various places in Denmark. One of the most far-reaching of these is taking place around the Tvind centres in Jutland. None of them receives very much support from official quarters.

This situation should be radically changed and new experiments started over a wide front, particularly where they can be based on local initiative. There should be as few restrictions imposed on these experiments as possible, although in order to serve the goal we have in view, the following basic requirements must be fulfilled:

1. All employees should have a voice in determining conditions in the enterprise.
2. All employees should receive the same hourly wage.
3. The board of directors must be composed of representatives from the employees, the local community and the state.
4. The management should be democratically elected by all employees.
5. Any profit must be used solely for investment in the enterprise or for public purposes.

Companies which follow these basic rules are called cooperative enterprises. They are free to adopt workers' resolutions concerning forms of work, working hours, the size of production teams, working environment, choices of technological methods and so on.

To set this new development in motion, a new administrative office (here called the Industrial Development Office) should be created in the Ministry of Industry. With a small staff and sizeable funds, the new office will work in consultation with local politicians to approve experimental enterprises and to ensure that the approved companies follow the proposed basic rules. New activities should be the result of interaction between local initiative and the central Industrial Development Office. The central office must interfere as little as possible in the day to day running of the enterprises. The office's funds are used to make investment loans to approved enterprises. New enterprises receive these loans interest-free for the first five years after which interest payments can be graduated upwards over the next five year period to a maximum rate (say 10%).

During the first 10 years of operations, all funding for the industrial loan scheme will have to be voted through on the annual finance Bill. Later, funds will automatically flow in, partly from interest payments and partly from private production capital reverting to the state on the owner's death. Once the process has been set in motion, it could turn the present system of capitalist production into a system of society/employee controlled production within a couple of generations. The first step is always the hardest, however, and the initial ten years will be the critical period in this scheme. Let us examine some of the immediate problems.

How is the development of new production structures to begin? Will there, for example, be any existing firms interested in joining the experiment when they have to fulfil the basic rules we have drawn up? Not many to start with. On the other hand, it will be an advantage if the new structures are not introduced solely in new enterprises, and several possibilities could be suggested. For example, there is the small family firm which is facing demands for relatively large new investment and a change in ownership to the next generation. Experience shows that firms like this are frequently bought up by some larger company in the same line of business. Following our action programme, the industrial development office should become actively involved and offer to buy out the private owners, allowing the employees to take over the firm in accordance with the basic rules.

Then there is the firm which is forced by competition to introduce new, labour-saving technology or go out of business. This problem, which is closely linked to rising structural unemployment, appears almost insoluble within the existing capitalist system. Following our action programme, the industrial development office should intervene and offer the employees an opportunity to take over both the firm and the problem of introducing new technology with a plan which pays as much regard as possible to the interests of the employees. If the basic rules are obeyed, responsibility for planning will lie chiefly with the firm's new board of directors composed of representatives from the workforce, the local community and the state; a triad much better qualified to deal with the tasks in hand than the present type of management which is dominated by private economic interests.

A third kind of company which might be included here is the capital intensive firm planning to introduce new production based on highly advanced technology. The rate of technological development often results in such firms selling themselves to a foreign multinational in order to solve the problem of capital requirements. This trend works directly against the desire for a home-based manufacturing structure which considers the interests of workers and local community first and foremost. Here, too, the industrial development office should intervene; and here too, our action programme comes into direct conflict with the interests of international capital.

Who will be taking part in the experiment? It is hardly likely that existing Western firms will be queuing for a place in the experimental production programme, even if the industrial development office is offering them cheap investment loans. On the other hand, there will probably be sufficient interest among existing firms to give the programme reasonable support from the start.

Further cooperation will come chiefly from new manufacturing groups, and interest in the experimental programme will be heightened by the large unemployment figures. It is important that the industrial development office provides expert consultative assistance for these new manufacturing groups. But it is equally important that we face the fact from the very beginning that some of these experiments will fail, for technical or human reasons. Our present political system is not very tolerant of public institutions which invest money in unsuccessful projects. The industrial development office will therefore have to make it quite clear when drawing up its programme that some proportion of its investment funds may well have to be used to cover losses from unsuccessful experiments. For psychological reasons, however, the office would be advised to invest the bulk of its funds during the first ten year period in projects with a reasonable chance of survival.

Considering the present unemployment problem and the vast unemployment among young people in particular, it should be possible to win political support for the kind of programme we describe. It is crucial, however, that the programme should not simply paper over the cracks to conform with traditional capitalist and union premisses. If it is to have a wider significance, the new programme must start from an entirely new set of basic principles. The proposals we have submitted might possibly serve as a starting point for the formation of the new rules.

Official industrial policy should be oriented more towards support for something akin to the 'intermediate technology' discussed by Schumacher in *Small is Beautiful*.

Intermediate technology consists of technology which is simple, easy to understand and maintain, relatively cheap, chiefly dependent on local resources and suited to local needs. It is more labour-intensive than capital-intensive, and the manufacturing processes it employs do not damage the environment. In short, it is appropriate to human and environmental needs rather than technical and commercial needs.

Examples of intermediate technology in present circumstances might include solar heating systems, windmills, biomass systems, efficient central heating boilers able to use coal, oil and gas, new forms of insulation for existing housing and so on.

Some passing remarks on mobility of capital. Given our objectives, we obviously cannot allow control of a significant part of businesses built up in any one country to be transferred abroad; any more than we can allow private capital accumulated at home and based on the work of indigenous citizens in the manufacturing and service sectors to be freely transferable to other countries at the whim of the private capitalist. At the moment capital transfers of this sort have to be approved in most countries by their national banks. If our aims are to be achieved, permission should only be granted in special cases after the interests of society as a whole have been taken into account. If international developments within the EEC were to allow free capital transfers, then our future society would have to withdraw from the international agreement in question. This is a major factor in safeguarding the planned social development.

During the transitional phase, the banks and insurance companies which exercise an influence over a considerable part of new investment in industry will occupy a key position. There will have to be loyal support from the finance system in order to secure a flexible transition to the new production structure with its state-owned cooperative enterprises. Otherwise the only solution will be state control of the whole finance system.

There will also need to be strict legislation against unilateral business closures so that viable firms can continue as cooperative enterprises. There is little doubt that the transitional phase will create many conflicts of interest, but there is still an enormous gap between the measures we suggest and revolution in the traditional sense. In our programme, existing capitalists are given a period in which to wind up affairs slowly and systematically, the only requirement being that they do not make arrangements that conflict with the long term objective. Should it transpire that the majority of capitalists and employers refuse to work towards public ownership nonetheless, then the new production structure will just have to be introduced more rapidly than planned. And that would not be an attrative proposition for either side. In addition to the transitional measures already mentioned, there will also have to be an automatic mechanism ensuring that over the long term all large companies acquire the status of cooperative enterprises. One way of achieving this might be by transferring an increasing share of company profits to the state but leaving them in the company as publicly owned assets.

During the transitional phase, cooperative enterprises will have to compete with traditional firms in an almost free market. In all probability, therefore, they cannot afford to give lower priority to productivity straight away. On the other hand there is no reason to suppose that a cooperative enterprise with a free and democratically organized structure and a motivated work force should be less competitive than a firm managed according to traditional and more authoritarian principles. References to bad experiences among nationalized companies in some countries are not really relevant here since they are not in fact organized as cooperative enterprises.

Experiments in new lifestyles. To judge from various experiments in Scandinavia and elsewhere, there would appear to be a clear connection between new lifestyles and new forms of production. Until now society has been more intolerant towards experiments in new lifestyles than towards experiments in production. The establishment reacts to social experiments of this kind by threatening to demolish the site. What the politicians ought to be doing is offering support to a whole range of experiments in new kinds of community living so that wider practical experience can be gained of potential living patterns. This support could consist of direct grants or tax allowances and rent rebates, but it is important that any subsidies are subject to as few conditions as possible.

PREPARING FOR ACTIVE LOCAL DEMOCRACY

It is not necessary to make major changes in the existing political structure in order to practise active local democracy. One of the preconditions for active local democracy is that people should be familiar with the problems under discussion and with the men and women they elect to represent them in any further debate on the matter. Political activities must therefore seek their point of departure in local questions affecting the daily life of the citizen, and the political election process must begin in the local community where everyone knows something about everyone else. In Chapter IV we described a political structure which makes allowances for these objectives. In the new system, the local community, the municipality and the state are all involved in the political process and the present county system has been dropped. A great deal can be done, however, to improve local democracy before the new framework is established. It is important that we build up a practical foundation as soon as possible.

There are many ways in which local democracy could be strengthened. For some years now, experiments have been conducted with local citizens' committees, joint cultural councils and so on. In many cases it has proved difficult for activities of this kind to function properly within a political system which does not look too favourably upon 'unofficial' political initiative. It is imperative that the work of local democracy be encouraged by according it a more recognized status.

The system of citizens' councils described below is one possibility; many other alternatives could be suggested. The aim in view must be that individual communities are given a chance to experiment with different structures.

The present political structure in Denmark is built on a system of town councils, county councils and parliament, each with their own area of competence. Similar structures exist in many other countries. One way to strengthen local democracy might be by setting up various forms of citizens' councils alongside the existing structure and giving them real powers to deal with selected issues. Actual powers have a crucial effect in motivating the citizen to make the necessary effort and in forcing the 'professional' politicians to listen to the citizens.

The basic units in our proposed system are the local communities, which may on average number about 1,000 people (around 300 families), and preferably not many more if everyone is to be able to know everyone else. A local community might consist of a village, a group of single family houses, a collection of apartment buildings and so on. What matters is that the community boundaries should be worked out in a natural way to suit the locality. Every group of this kind can then register itself as a local community. The members are those local people who wish to take part. Meetings of community members take place whenever there is a need to discuss common activities and events involving the area.

Each local community in the municipality chooses a representative to sit on the municipal citizens' council. For practical purposes the large municipalities will need to be split into smaller subdivisions, each with their own citizens' council. The local representative ensures that the local community is kept informed of municipal plans and projects early enough for the community to influence further developments.

Apart from the local community representatives, the municipal citizens' council may also include representatives from associations, clubs, societies, etc. in the municipality, thereby ensuring that a broad spectrum of cultural interests is accommodated in the active work of local democracy. There will also be opportunities for the town council to entrust management of certain cultural activities in the municipality to the citizens' council.

The citizens' council could be responsible for following the work of the town council and organizing public hearings and civic meetings to discuss local plans. A number of town councils are already sponsoring civic meetings, but the citizens have seldom been able to exercise any real influence on decisions which have already been planned by a majority in the council. It is often held that reforms in local democracy should under no circumstances undermine the efficiency of the town council. Given this basic requirement, there is little room left for new forms of local democracy. Many people regard the official moves and experiments conducted so far in this field as purely symbolic, and they have gathered together into non-party-political citizens' and environmental groups putting up their own candidates for local elections, since they see this as the only method of exerting any influence. This is a positive and logical development, but it has proved difficult for citizens' groups to compete with traditional party coalitions in most municipalities. That is one of the reasons why it is important to create a system of citizens' councils and to give these councils real political powers. These must include the right of citizens' councils to demand that town councils refer questions on which the two parties disagree to local referenda.

There is little danger that traditional party-political divisions would penetrate the citizens' council because local community elections would be based on a personal vote. Furthermore, no one should be allowed to sit on both the citizens' council and the town council.

Citizens' council members will come to feel far more like political 'amateurs', tied to the grass roots, unlike many 'professional' town council members who feel more drawn by signals from party headquarters by the time they reach the second half of their term in office. It is for this very reason that citizens' councils are so badly needed.

The citizens' council system can be pursued through to county level by setting up a regional citizens' council alongside every county council. This regional citizens' council would consist of representatives from each municipal citizens' council in the county and would be given similar powers in its dealings with the county council. The case for carrying the system of citizens' councils through to parliamentary level is not so clear cut. This is partly because parliament is bound to concern itself with overall social questions which cut across community and municipal boundaries. Even so, important aspects of the general idea can be applied at this level; there is just as much need to restore the people's confidence here. The crucial question when it comes to establishing a national citizens' council of this kind alongside parliament must relate to its powers and its composition. As far as powers are concerned, the same ideas could be applied here as to the other citizens' councils, namely that the national citizens' council should act to control and inspire parliament, should be in charge of public hearings and should be able to demand referenda.

When it comes to composition of the council, efforts must be made to ensure that the national citizens' council complements parliament and is not just a party-political copy of it. Most importantly of all, the council must be composed in such a way that it firmly counterbalances the trend towards centralized and excessive tutelage from above.

Given these requirements, we would suggest that for a country of the size of Denmark a national citizens' council be set up with about 120 members, half of whom represent the regional councils (four for each and an extra four for the Capital). The other half would consist of representatives from the largest trade organizations, professional societies, trade unions, cultural associations, environmental groups, etc., elected by members of these organizations on a four-yearly ballot. The national citizens' council could be a forerunner for the professional assembly to be introduced when the system changes, as described in Chapter IV. In a similar way the municipal citizens' councils could be gathering experience with a view to the future municipal assembly.

If citizens' councils were introduced alongside the present structures at these three levels, there would be some hope of bringing a new dimension to the political system, a dimension which might counteract the crisis of confidence under which the existing system is now working. The new citizens' councils could also inspire more active political commitment in the local community, and create additional channels of interaction between the grass roots and the central political assemblies.

Very few constitutional changes will be needed to institute experimental citizens' councils of this kind, and our traditional democratic principles will not be affected. On the contrary, such an experiment could eventually be the salvation of our representative democracy.

POLITICAL INFORMATION AT NATIONAL LEVEL

The relationship between politicians and the mass media must be changed from one of mutual mistrust to one of professional collaboration.
It is much easier to make active democracy work as it should in relation to local issues, i.e. in the local community and municipality. When it comes to national and international politics, the problems are often so complicated and abstract that many people are deterred from pursuing the issue from the outset.

Even so, the political system ought to be able to deal with national and international questions on the basis of an enlightened, democratic decision-making process. This can only be achieved if parliament reorganizes its method of operations.

The most important facets of change would entail parliament spending far more time on coherent debates of political principle based on solid information, using the mass media as a continuous disseminator of information, and establishing closer contact with the people through advisory referenda and through constant gathering of proposals and comments from local communities and individual persons.

Instead of being exploited in a hectic and superficial way during the short pre-election period as television is now, the broadcasting services should provide a regular framework for programmes on fundamental political topics, preferably in conjunction with parliamentary debates on questions of principle. Among other things, this would entail broadcasting staffs (and politicians) devoting time to preparatory work so that the issues under discussion could be placed in a wider political context. It would also prompt the various political parties to explain how their programmes hang together.

Obviously it is an ambitious undertaking to change the workings of parliament and media as we suggest: so ambitious, indeed, that the effort required will be comparable with the work television puts into its expensive entertainment programmes. In order to deal with politics, television will have to employ a number of staff with expert knowledge of the major areas of the political arena and ensure that they are given enough time to carry out the necessary research for their broadcasts in collaboration with external advisers of various political convictions. At the same time there will have to be a change in attitude among politicians so that they are far more open in their dealings with the public: this means public access to committee meetings, official figures and analyses drawn up by the government administration and so on. Tactical secretiveness merely helps to increase the electorate's mistrust of political work.

Political discussions and hearings make good televisual material. It is a matter of obliging the television corporations to take on the job and granting the necessary funds. If television broadcasts are then followed up in the press, active national democracy should move a few steps closer to self-realization.

A GENERAL RATIONALIZATION OF THE COMPLEX OF LAWS

The civil service exists for the citizens. This principle should be observed in practice by both legislators and public servants. Personal freedom can be restricted in many ways. Unintentional though it is, legislation and administration between them have created a number of obstacles to individual fulfilment. The resultant animosity and frustration are so great that in Denmark a sizeable new protest party has come into being. It is time parliament did something about this problem. The most logical solution would be to set aside two years for a radical rationalization of the whole complex of laws. Any law that results in restrictions on personal freedom should be examined to see whether these restrictions are really necessary. If they are not, the law concerned should be amended or repealed.

In addition all laws should be examined in the light of their economic effect and their legitimacy in relation to legislation dealing with adjacent spheres in terms of both technicality and ideology. Certain laws today appear to work directly against one another. The legal jungle they create must be rationalized according to the criteria already mentioned.

Perhaps the most important task lies on the purely human level. This concerns the attitudes of public employees who administer the laws in daily contact with the people.

Although the concept of the 'desk-general' helps to create a distorted picture of public employees, there is enough truth in it to warrant efforts to change it. Human warmth, understanding and humility are often lacking in many of the public services. A different attitude is needed. Legislative rules and regulations relating to employment alone will not be enough to change attitudes, but there are various ways in which the prospects for change can be improved. One of these is to relax demands for educational qualifications: it is time that narrow organizational interests were broken down. Another measure might be to introduce more frequent role-changing so that public servants periodically change places with people in private business.

EMPLOYMENT PROBLEMS

Unemployment is a lack of solidarity. In the humane, ecologically sustainable society the work that needs to be done is shared out in solidarity. In the Western world today forced unemployment is an increasing scourge. Its repercussions on society are too serious for us to be able to wait 25 years or more for a solution. Apart from human considerations, the problem also requires an urgent solution because the safeguarding of jobs is being used as an excuse to continue a number of activities with harmful side effects: pollution and other kinds of environmental damage, bad working conditions and the development of new military systems. Parliament must therefore adopt new initiatives in this area and be given stronger powers to deal with employers and unions.

The most effective first move would be a demand for an overall reduction in working hours, by say 5% in the first instance, with a corresponding reduction in wages. At the same time all major employers (both private and public) should be obliged to take on 5% more workers. Once these measures had begun to take effect the reduction in wages could be partially offset by tax relief funded by savings in unemployment pay no longer given to those now working again. Low wage earners should be compensated for their wage reductions straight away by equivalent tax relief.

Some employers maintain that even today it is impossible to find labour for many jobs and that this is partly due to the laxity with which the benefit system is administered. However, this argument can in no way be used as an excuse to do nothing about the unemployment problem. On the contrary, it will be easier to correct possible flaws in the benefit system when jobs are in reasonable supply once again.

For the sake of the many young unemployed in particular, effective solutions are urgently needed. The cosmetic job that has been applied so far has proved far too ineffectual, however well meant. If a 5% reduction in working hours is not enough, the percentage must be increased until there is full employment. This line of action is entirely in keeping with the proposed principles for the future society.

In addition to the overall measures, special arrangements can be made for those trades or professions particularly hard hit by unemployment. Considerable unemployment is forecast, for example, among several categories of university graduates for the next few decades. Attempts could be made to counteract this trend now by arranging that all newly employed graduates in the public sector worked reduced hours. The number of hours worked, say two thirds or one half of the normal working week, would have to depend on prognoses and actual trends and could be adjusted at suitable intervals. What matters is that the basic principle involves solidarity in solving the problem, so that a large group of people do not have to see the value of their lengthy education deteriorating in idleness. Similar measures could be used in other trades and professions. Society ought also to make further use of jobs in the public service sectors. The large numbers of unemployed are paid by the state in any case, only they may not work for their pay. The thinking behind arguments against expanding the public sector belongs to a society where there is no unemployment. To meet these arguments new appointments could be made for limited periods (three years for example) with allowances for flexibility if there should be an (unexpected) labour shortage. If it were further advocated that temporary jobs of this kind should be on a part-time basis so that wages were equivalent to unemployment pay there would be no extra cost to the state over all. The human and social benefits of this principle are obvious, and narrow organizational interests should not be allowed to block development along these lines.

Apart from the points already mentioned which are aimed specifically at sharing existing work more fairly, moves could also be made to create new jobs. This could happen through various forms of aid to industry (risk capital, better provision for depreciation, export subsidies, public development contracts, new forms of manufacturing centres specially for the young, etc.). Although these possibilities ought to be exploited, there is no avoiding the fact that all industrial nations will be trying to produce their way out of unemployment. This trend may easily result in the most efficient countries exporting their unemployment to the less efficient. Each country would therefore do well to recognize the limitations of these measures as soon as possible.

EDUCATION FOR A HUMANE, SUSTAINABLE SOCIETY

Specific political parties in many Western societies have succeeded in making academics unpopular among the people – not entirely unaided by the academics themselves. In the proposed future society this cannot occur. Partly because no well-defined academic group will exist and partly because no form of education will give anyone special advantages.

In preparing an educational structure suited to the future society our primary objective must be to break down existing, rigid divisions between professions and to remove the distinctions between theoretical and practical education. Ideas of this kind have already been floated in education debates and a few tentative steps along these lines are being taken in primary schools. But generally speaking there has been no more than these tentative efforts, and in recent years they have been so faltering that it is hard to see whether they are moving in the right direction at all. The old hierarchical school ideas are still very much in force.

Educational reforms intended to meet the requirements of the future society must balance theoretical knowledge with practical work experience in all kinds of education and at every level. Not in the form of superficial visits to factories and institutions, but as an integral part of education and of sufficient length in time for pupils to get a real feel for working conditions. There must be a steady increase in opportunities for children to deal with real life, not just to prepare for it. They must handle things themselves.

Society, industry, public institutions of all kinds must assume joint responsibility here. If they cannot provide places enough for young trainees, opportunities for handling real work problems must be created within the educational framework.

A look at what has been achieved in experiments where young people are building houses, erecting windmills, manufacturing furniture, working in fishery, agriculture, horticulture and so on, without much expert professional assistance, leaves no doubt that the necessary switch in the education sector can be made.

We must assume that in the future, as now, only a minority of the young will go on to further education. Even with closer links between school and practical work there will still be a dividing line between the more highly educated minority and the rest of the population which will have to be broken down. One way of achieving this in the longer term will be by demanding that students spend at least one year in practical work between leaving school and starting further education. In addition, more advanced studies should include periods of practical work, preferably affiliated to the professional field in question.

All work done by trainees, from primary school to university level, should be paid. Levels of pay for younger children can be token wages (subsidized pocket money). It is an important matter of principle to emphasize through some form of wage that even children are able to make a valuable contribution to the work of society. Younger children would be paid by the state. For older trainees the firm would pay an increasing proportion of the wage.

The integration of education and work is an essential measure in preparations for the future society and must be central to the political action programme.

EXPERTS AND TECHNOLOGY ASSESSMENT

The power of the anonymous expert is an obstacle to democracy. The real
source of that endless stream of Bills which pour out of the central
offices of government is impossible to trace. They are produced,
so it is said, with the help of experts. The anonymous, hand-
picked experts of central government. The members of parliament do not know them, the government hardly knows them
either. The experts are not politically accountable, but they are
politically significant. When they make their rare public appear-
ances it is usually to defend the existing system and traditional
development. Only in connection with particularly controversial
subjects can the experts be made to reveal their own differences
of opinion to the public. The nuclear energy debate is a current
example of this. The majority of experts appear to think that
nuclear energy is too complex a question for the layman to make
judgments about. Most experts, in fact, take the same position in
relation to virtually all controversial subjects within their field
of specialization. Experts can therefore imperil democracy and
impede the trend towards the kind of broad political involvement
which is basic to the humane, sustainable society. The best
weapon against the power of the expert is openness. Expert
evaluations and recommendations for new legislation, new
technological projects and so on must therefore be made totally
accessible to the public. The experts must be available to attend
public hearings when called on by the citizens' councils and other
civic groups. And the citizens must be able to draw on 'alternative' experts of varying political persuasions.

Some progress along these lines is beginning to occur in the
U.S.A. In Denmark there have been occasional activities of
this kind. In 1976, for example, there was a public hearing on
government energy plans and alternative energy plans.

Many of these questions involve the concept of technology
assessment which includes a systematic analysis of the economic,
environmental and social consequences of new technology. The
idea is that technology assessment should be carried out before
new technology is let loose on society. The political philosophy
underlying this idea is that technological development should be
suited to people's needs, and not the reverse. One means of

achieving this is to use technology assessment systematically in connection with the political decision-making process. Another is to impose a statutory obligation to make the results of technology assessment public and provide opportunities for public hearings with the participation of 'alternative' experts, preferably on television.

Without these and other measures the ordinary citizen will tend to lose out in confrontations with the experts, whether the projects concerned be national or local

ENVIRONMENTAL PROBLEMS

If we wait too long there will be no environment left to sustain. Danish legislation on the environment is described as the best in the world – by the politicians who created it. Perhaps they are right. But in that case it is all the more sad that it has so many flaws in practice. One evident shortcoming is that the environment law is very much like an emergency powers act and that the emergency powers it grants appear so far to have been applied to minor problems while many of the major problems are allowed to pass by unchallenged. Thus it is possible for large industrial companies to start by producing a great deal of pollution and then to set up new divisions for the development of anti-pollution methods. They have experience in the field, after all, and the whole process produces economic growth.

Another basic shortcoming is that whenever local employment interests conflict with local environmental interests, the environment nearly always loses. And whenever there is a confrontation between technological development (in the form of freeways, high voltage lines, supermarkets, tourist hotels, airports, bridges, etc.) and groups seeking to preserve areas of natural beauty, the environment again loses. In the main this is because the people protecting the environment have neither the political nor the economic resources required at their disposal. The progenitors of the 'best legislation on the environment in the world' have failed to see that it takes considerable economic and political resources to preserve and protect the natural environment. Well-meaning decisions of principle are not enough.

We need intervention on two fronts. A solution to the unemployment problem will eliminate conflicts of interest between the environment and job preservation. In addition, rapid action must be taken to provide much larger grants from public funds for the preservation or purchase of natural areas threatened with ruthless building development or in danger of being bought up by financially strong EEC neighbours.

This line of development is perfectly in keeping with preliminary moves towards the future ownership of land by society. If the political will is there the community will be able to make compulsory purchase and preservation orders without high expenditure. It makes no sense that people should still be able to make large profits on amenities created by nature or the community. Besides, the present system contributes to the rise in inflation and makes it very expensive for young people with low incomes to acquire a home.

During the transitional phase it is also important that the environment ministry acts as a body of specialist support for local environment groups against the often very short-sighted projects of established circles. The idea that a ministry should support action which might be described as 'extra-parliamentary' is a new departure from established thinking. But the staff at the environment ministry should be the first to understand a new departure of this kind.

THE EXPLOITATION OF LIMITED RAW MATERIALS

Save and recycle is the way forward – and this applies to energy as well. The supplier of renewable solar energy charges nothing for it. In the future society we have chosen to rely on renewable energy sources, primarily solar energy. Production has been systematically built up with a view to recycling metal, glass, paper, etc., and with a view to making products as durable as possible. In the future society the repairs industry has regained its old respect and value.

These ideas are also given an airing in the political debates of today and there is much talk of energy saving. Governments have spent money on flashy television campaigns for saving energy without any measurable result. If the way in which society uses energy is to be radically changed then such campaigns without commitment are not the right way to go about it. If, on the other hand, the people are given evidence that their efforts have some real significance they are willing to make sacrifices, as the 1973 oil crisis showed. This can only be done by systematic long term planning which clearly illustrates to the people what can be achieved. Only if government and parliament take the lead with consistent legislation will there be a national effort based on broad public support.

Legislation should be initiated within the next few years and must concentrate on the four major areas of energy consumption: heating, transport, manufacturing and electricity. It is already quite clear what *ought* to be done. Since the political will still appears to be wavering, it may perhaps be valuable to reiterate some of the means.

Building regulations must be made far stricter than the provisions laid down in 1977. By 1983 standards of insulation should match those in the 'zero-energy house' at the Technical University of Denmark. By 1986 requirements should be set at an even higher level. These new laws must be passed now so that the building industry has time to adjust.

In the field of transport, the major consumers of energy are private cars. Since it is hardly possible to deprive people of their cars, discriminatory taxation in the form of registration duty must be introduced at short notice. Cars doing relatively few miles to the gallon should be subject to a much higher percentage of purchase tax than cars achieving a high mileage to the gallon. Consumers will doubtless react as they are meant to if taxation is sufficiently slanted against waste. Over 10-20 years car parks will come to look quite different. They will be dominated by small cars with efficient engines that drive at least 60 miles to the gallon.

The Danish manufacturing sector has relatively little heavy industry and accounts for a smaller proportion of gross national energy consumption than that in most industrialized countries. There is generally little economic incentive for individual firms to introduce energy-saving measures. From a national economic viewpoint the effect on the balance of payments is sufficiently significant for government to take a rapid lead over industry by bringing in regulations and investment subsidies to promote more efficient uses of energy.

Finally there is electricity consumption which has risen more steeply than other forms of energy consumption over the past decades, aided and abetted by a great deal of advertising from the electrical utility companies. This has resulted, among other things, in a significant rise over recent years in the number of new houses being built with electric heating. Considering that only about one third of the fuel value is used in electricity production, it would seem to be little short of wastefulness to use a high quality form of energy like electricity for such primitive purposes as low temperature heating.

If we are to stake our future on renewable energy sources and not on nuclear power, there is no immediate chance that electricity will be in plentiful supply. It should therefore only be used where necessary. There must be legislation against domestic electric heating and electrical equipment in houses and factories must be subject to much stricter energy-saving requirements.

In addition, it is possible to take measures which will result in a general energy-saving by imposing a heavy duty on primary energy. This suggestion has been brought up in parliament on several occasions but has been rejected for various suspect reasons, including the claim that industry would become less competitive. The truth is that in most places industry could easily improve its energy efficiency to the extent that the cost of the proposed duty became insignificant, and allowances could be made for the few industries unable to do that. The overall effect would be a greater saving of energy and a more healthy balance of trade.

There is little hope of renewable energy sources providing the bulk of our energy unless considerable efforts are made by the government. Far too much money is invested in the nuclear power industry which has already gone a long way to planning a system based on the 'plutonium economy'. Plutonium is to be the primary fuel in a number of mammoth nuclear power plants (fast breeder reactors), and because of the uncomfortable possibility of reactor disasters and of plutonium being misused to make nuclear weapons, society will be required to make an unprecedented contribution to the guarding and supervision of these reactors. The prospects before us have recently been examined in two official British reports. The Flowers Report says 'Our consideration of these matters, however, has led us to the view that we should not rely for energy supply on a process that produces such a hazardous substance as plutonium unless there is no reasonable alternative.' A similarly cautious note is sounded by Paul Sieghart in his capacity as chairman of an international legal committee. Sieghart concludes that 'the easiest path towards a police state in any modern society which is not one already, would be for that society to opt for a plutonium economy' (*The Times*, 2 August 1977).

A society reliant on nuclear power and a plutonium economy will obviously block the way to a humane, sustainable society. The alternative is to opt for renewable energy sources, in particular solar energy. We will have to make a considerable effort if renewable energy sources are to be an alternative to nuclear power. Fortunately renewable energy sources offer considerable short term advantages: more jobs, less use of foreign currency and greater reliability of supplies.

It should therefore be possible to make it a broad national programme to develop renewable energy sources in a form that suits the country concerned. And to ensure that there are sizeable public subsidies to back the rapid introduction and expansion of such energy use during the difficult initial phase when private economies do not constitute incentive enough for the liberalist system to change track.

When it comes to recycling, we must pass quickly beyond the present stage where random, small-scale projects are undertaken on a private or municipal basis. Most recycling firms will be vulnerable to fluctuations in the prices of raw materials. They will find it difficult to manage on purely private economic terms, regardless of social gain. A recycling industry should therefore be established with public involvement on the basis of special concern for the environment, for securing supplies and for employment.

SMALL NATIONS IN THE INTERNATIONAL CONTEXT

Being small is no excuse, especially if you are rich and well-educated. Working alone, countries like Denmark cannot solve the problems of the developing nations. They cannot abolish the atom bomb and bring about world disarmament. They cannot safeguard human rights and eliminate social injustice in other countries. So, is there any point in their having a foreign and security policy? It is certainly politically and economically convenient to treat foreign policy as purely symbolic, or at best as being limited to narrow, short-sighted national interests.

The error of pursuing this line of action is that narrow, short-sighted policies do not safeguard international interests. National security problems are directly bound up with world security problems. The possibilities of a country like Denmark independently developing a new social system are closely connected with the ability to win understanding and approval for the sense of its plans from international collaborators.

Were Denmark, for example, to attempt the transition to a humane, sustainable society, it would be much easier if the other Scandinavian countries and some of its EEC partners set themselves similar goals or at least regarded the Danish experiment in a sympathetic light. As far as the EEC is concerned, any member nation attempting political change along the lines we suggest would have to retain total control over transfers of capital out of the country during the transitional phase. There is no reason why this should restrict freedom of trade, so it should be acceptable even to the more conservative EEC members. The question still remains, however, whether traditional, liberalist philosophers will continue to dominate the EEC. If such is the case the EEC will persist in its attempts to force a more open economy on member countries so that large-scale industry and the multinational companies can make the most productive use of their capital resources. There are signs that the EEC is coming to a new point of departure on this issue, if for no other reason than that the socialist parties are becoming increasingly influential within some member countries.

Any EEC members which decide to work towards our proposed goals will have to start by winning approval in Europe for measures that will facilitate change although no nation can either demand or expect that its EEC partners will accept arrangements of unilateral benefit to the country in question. If national experiments prove successful, then efforts must be made to create interest in similar systems among international working partners.

In the event that the EEC is unable to tolerate a member country experimenting with new political structures then that country will have to take the consequences. The benefits of membership are already increasingly open to doubt in some countries.

Whatever the future composition of the EEC, efforts should be made now to broaden its activities and alter its perspectives. The following examples indicate some of the areas in which change is to be advocated:

1. The EEC must avoid policies which mark it as a rich man's club turning its back on the poor. Instead the community must take a lead in furthering international detente and pressing for a new economic world order which considers the legitimate claims of the developing nations.

2. The administrative theories of the EEC should be changed so that present trends towards centralization are reversed and devolution becomes the objective. Only those problems which cannot be solved nationally should be carried forward to EEC level.

3. The EEC should work actively to ensure respect for human rights all over the world. This could be underlined by a special EEC declaration to be binding on the member states.

4. The EEC must change its very traditional energy policy and invest in renewable energy sources to a far greater extent, working harder at the same time on energy conservation measures.

5. The EEC must help to strengthen small and medium sized businesses through administrative measures and a research and development policy that pays particular attention to their needs.

6. The EEC must make a more active effort to protect the environment. Larger funds must be set aside to safeguard the quality of life for future generations.

7. The aim of EEC agricultural policy should be to satisfy world needs and to preserve ways of life important to human development at home. EEC agricultural policy should be related to the long-term policies of the developing countries in this sphere.

THE NEW ECONOMIC WORLD ORDER

The small wealthy nations can play a special part in changing the present discriminatory world order. In his report to the Club of Rome in 1976, J. Tinbergen emphasized the importance of establishing a strong element of neutrality and automatic procedure in the provision of aid to developing countries, particularly in relation to the poorest regions where people are living on or under the hunger line. One of the proposed means of achieving this is an international duty or tax on the consumption of natural resources, e.g. in the sea. The proceeds could then be administered by an international body linked to the UN.

The fundamental thinking behind this proposal appears eminently reasonable and the principle should be extended to national areas. The natural resources scattered haphazardly across the globe should be regarded on principle as the common inheritance and property of mankind. It is unreasonable that one group of people who happen to be living on a piece of land rich in mineral deposits should therefore take these minerals as their patrimony and determine at what rate and to what extent they should be exploited. Since the concept of private property is still sacrosanct in most places (amongst the property owners in any case), it is bound to take time before the idea of common ownership is accepted throughout the world. On the other hand, there is more likely to be acceptance for a certain level of duty on everybody once the owners have received reasonable financial compensation for their work in the exploitation of resources.

Many Western European nations have no particular traditions in the exploitation of natural raw materials, and for good reason. But this state of affairs is bound to change over the next decade with the discovery of oil and gas in the North Sea. It would make a real psychological impact if countries like Denmark were to voluntarily undertake payment of an international duty on their resources (say 10% of the turnover) before they had even obtained a total survey of their mineral deposits. The proceeds could be administered by an international body as Tinbergen proposes. At the same time these countries could make an active endeavour in the EEC, the OECD and the UN to get other states to follow their example, though this should not be a precondition for their initiative. This kind of policy towards the developing nations would have far-reaching prospects despite the fact that it has been initiated by a small country with little direct influence.

In addition the smaller, wealthy nations should do more to make themselves assertive spokesmen for the views of the developing nations on the form and extent of aid from industrial countries. We should be seeking improved trade conditions for developing nations, increased and stabilized prices for raw materials, larger capital transfers, collaboration over science and technology, etc. Some of these points have been dealt with earlier in this book.

SECURITY POLICY

400,000 (40%) of the world's engineers and scientists are working on the development and production of armaments. Who is working to prevent conflict? If armed conflict were to break out on a global scale there would no longer be a basis for the humane, sustainable society. This threat hangs over every attempt at political development. The question is whether we should simply put the possibility out of our minds as best we can, or face it and try to prevent it. The standard response from many European politicians is a reference to NATO and to the fact that small countries cannot do very much.

However, security policy means more than military alliances and mutual defence agreements. Security policy is also a matter of creating stable social and economic conditions, of safeguarding access to vital foods, energy and other resources, of reducing the gap between the poor countries and the rich, and it is very much a matter of securing the necessary information on which to base decisions in conflict situations. All too often states act in panic and ignorance because they lack the will or the means to keep themselves adequately informed in times of crisis. In such situations the international public is left high and dry by the mass media which concentrate mainly on 'news' and cannot supply the continuous and unbiased explanation of events which is a prerequisite for the professional evaluation and possible prevention of imminent conflict.

Neither the UN nor any other international institution has

succeeded in creating a permanent body able to perform this important function. It was in the light of this that in 1968 Denmark moved a proposal, since supported by the international Pugwash movement, that a supranational council be set up to gather and explore facts related to the trend of current conflicts and regions of tension. The council was to be independent of all national and international authorities and consist of 50 highly qualified experts. The council was also to be served by a secretariat employing a permanent staff which would ensure the greatest possible impartiality and objectivity. The secretariat was to suggest problems to the council and illustrate the practical possibilities for their solution; it was also to collaborate with other institutions working in the same field and present the results of the council's work to the world, and not just to the parties involved. There needs to be complete frankness about things which are traditionally kept secret and which are highly important for the security of the nations, possibly even for the future of all mankind. A motion that Denmark should take steps to examine the possibilities of setting up such a council was laid before parliament in 1972 but has been taken no further because of a sudden change in government. Since then it would appear that there have been more important matters claiming parliamentary time. In the context of security policy, however, it is difficult to imagine anything more important than reducing the chances of international conflict. This motion should therefore be re-adopted and both Denmark and other nations could quite properly grant a sum of money equivalent to 1% of their defence budget to be spent on this vital defensive work, starting with a five year period to test the viability of the idea.

The greatest danger to world peace is the accelerating arms race between the superpowers. By and large the long-standing disarmament talks have produced no tangible results and despite much talk of the superpowers having to concentrate their military efforts on defence systems, all the evidence suggests that the military leaders are doing exactly the opposite. In the eyes of the military strategist every weapons system can be described as defensive.

If this fatal race is to be influenced from outside, it is time the small countries used more aggressive tactics against the superpowers, especially as the small countries (particularly in Europe) are likely to become the primary battlefield in the initial phases of a military clash between the superpowers.

We need to unite the small nations in a demand for more knowledge and control of military developments among the superpowers. Details of wording could be discussed at international meetings and these should take place regardless of whether the larger nations agree to participate or not. One of the results would undoubtedly be a demand that the superpowers should truly exchange their offensive weapons for defensive systems. But this will not happen unless a broadly based pressure group comes into being and is able to use world opinion as one of its means of pressure. No one could decry an initiative of this kind as power politics. The potential victims of a world war must have a moral right to reduce the risk of their own annihilation: a right which the superpowers cannot in all decency deny unless they wish to be ostracized by the rest of the world.

The smaller nations could also make an active effort to stop the spread of nuclear power and the consequent possibilities of un-controlled atom-bomb manufacture. The major driving force in this dangerous process is short-sighted commercial competition between the individual countries that produce nuclear power stations.

REVOLT FROM THE CENTER

Only a few years ago a written programme like this would have seemed more provocative than it does now. The belief that it is possible to improve things without basically changing them was stronger then – and we were among the believers. Now, it is difficult to believe in any kind of change at all for the better. The Danish prime minister Anker Jørgensen has said that we 'will not get to heaven, but we shall try to avoid going to hell.' It is doubtful whether the efforts of the politicians will be crowned with success. Increasing economic difficulties will further limit our political freedom of action and exacerbate the conflicts in society. Once society has split down the middle, the way is open for 'solutions' that imperil democracy.

We anticipate that this appeal for a revolt from the center, or merely for a new departure from the center, will be regarded by the one side as extreme left wing and by the other as a petty bourgeois attempt to protect the established order. In that case we shall simply be confirmed in our major aim. But we do not wish to cut ourselves off from anyone: as we see it there is room enough in the 'middle' for a large democratic majority, the term being used here qualitatively rather than quantitatively. Democracy is the true middle ground between anarchic (group) self-ishness and totalitarian institutionalism. If the champions of democracy are on the defensive, a stalemate between extremes does not sustain democracy but undermines it. 'Face to face with the two anarchic extremes, democracy all too often forgets – and this is its weakness – that it, too, has a radicalism to represent: the radicalism of the center' (H. Broch).

Only a few years ago it was still generally believed that development would lead to further democracy – now there is greater reason to fear that democracy is only an episode in history. Few societies are democratic, democracy is under threat in several of them, and it is scarcely triumphant in any of them; the triumph of democracy is a utopian illusion. Democracy requires a radical break with prevailing development trends; but the goals of democracy are not so utopian as to make their demands on the present generation inhuman: on the contrary the demands are for humanity and solidarity, for solidarity, too, with the future generations whose conditions of life depend on what we do and fail to do. When we consider what the alternative is, we cannot accept that the democratic, ecologically sustainable society should be only a utopia.

BIBLIOGRAPHY

The following list contains only works which have been quoted in this book or those which have had a direct influence on the presentation of certain passages. Where such works have been translated into English the first English edition is included.

Poul Bjerre: Landsbypolitik – samfundspolitik. Dansk byplan-laboratoriums skriftserie 8, 1974.
Poul Bjerre: Demokrati som normalbegreb. 77 seminar om humanistisk politik.
Hermann Broch: Massenpsychologie, Zurich 1959.
Suzanne Brøgger: Deliver Us From Love, trans. Thomas Teal, London 1977.
Nils Christie: Hvor tett et samfunn? Copenhagen and Oslo 1975.
Jørgen S. Dich: Den herskende klasse, Copenhagen 1973.
Th. Dobzhansky: Genetic Diversity and Human Equality, 1973.
I. Eibl-Eibesfeldt: Love and Hate, trans. Geoffrey Strachan, London 1971.
J. K. Galbraith: The Affluent Society, London 1958.
         The New Industrial State, London 1967.
         Economics and the Public Purpose, London 1974.
Bertel Haarder: Statskollektivisme og spildproduktion, Copenhagen 1973.
Svante Iger: Den svenska ekonomins internationalisering, Rapport nr. 206 fra projektgruppen Sveriges internationella villkor, Secretariat for Future Studies, Stockholm 1976
Ivan Illich: Tools for Conviviality, London 1973.
Jacob Knudsen: Livsfilosofi, 4th edition, Copenhagen 1948.
Konrad Lorenz: On Aggression, London 1966.
         Behind the Mirror, London 1977.
Knud Lundberg: Født til et andet liv, Copenhagen 1976.

Ernest Mandel: Late Capitalism, trans. Joris de Bres, London 1975.

Herbert Marcuse: One-dimensional man. London 1968.

Karl Marx: Economic and Philosophic Manuscripts trans. Martin Mulligan, London 1959.

Fundamentals of Marxism-Leninism, ed. Otto Kuusinen, London 1961.

Jacques Monod: Chance and Necessity, trans. A. Wainhouse, London 1972.

Alva Myrdal and Frank Barnaby: in Development Dialogue, Dag Hammarskjöld Foundation, Uppsala 1977 (1).

Gunnar Myrdal: Challenge of World Poverty, London 1971.

Poul Møller: Politik paa vrangen, Copenhagen 1974.

Nuclear Power and the Environment, 6th Report from the Royal Commission on Environmental Pollution (chairman Brian Flowers), September 1976.

Arne Naess: Økologie, samfunn og livstil, Oslo 1976.

K. Helveg Petersen: Forslag om oprettelse af et internationalt raad for forskning og information om konflikter, Copenhagen 1971.

K. Helveg Petersen and others: Forslag til folketingsbeslutning om oprettelse af et fond til finansiering af saerlige sikkerheds-politiske initiativer. Folketinget 1972-1973, sheet No. 89.

Karl Henrik Pettersson: Reap the Whirlwind: Industrial Society uncontrolled, trans. W. Glyn Jones, London 1975.

E. F. Schumacher: Small is Beautiful, London 1973.

B. F. Skinner: Beyond Freedom and Dignity, London 1972.

Villy Sørensen: Uden maal – og med, Copenhagen 1973.

J. Tinbergen: Reshaping the International Order, New York, 1976.

Arnold Toynbee: Mankind and Mother Earth, New York and London 1976.

Max Weber: Protestant Ethic and the Spirit of Capitalism, trans. T. Parsons, London 1971.

Joseph Weizenbaum: Computer Power and Human Reason, San Francisco, 1976.

INDEX